Praise for
THE 10 COMMANDMENTS OF COMMON SENSE

"Like all the best advice, *The 10 Commandments of Common Sense* is simple but profound. Hal Urban has brought a lifetime's spiritual journey, a wide-ranging worldview, and an abundance of passion to bear on the matter of achieving a life well lived. And he succeeds. There is a better you to be found in this book."
—David Niven, Ph.D., author of *100 Simple Secrets of Happy People*

"*The 10 Commandments of Common Sense* is a recipe for happy and fulfilled living. By applying ancient wisdom to modern life, Hal Urban provides ten straightforward steps that can transform the life of any reader. It is an inspiration."
—Craig and Marc Kielburger, *New York Times* bestselling authors of *Me to We*

"Read this gem and let the power and truth of the Scriptures leap off the page and into your heart and everyday life. I especially loved the chapters on love, joy, and purpose."
—Jon Gordon, author of *Energy Addict* and *The Energy Bus*

"When Hal Urban writes a new book, I stop what I'm doing and start reading. You will too. *The 10 Commandments of Common Sense* is Hal's best one yet!"
—Pat Williams, senior vice president of the Orlando Magic

"In this book Hal Urban, a master teacher, has chosen ten lessons from the greatest book ever written to help readers become the best they can be."
—Sanford N. McDonnell, chairman emeritus of the Character Education Partnership, chairman emeritus of the McDonnell Douglas Corporation

"Hal Urban once again boils down wisdom into a quick, practical, and life-changing book. Read it and prosper."
—Laurie Beth Jones, author of *Jesus, CEO* and *The Path*

"Another wise and wonderful book from Hal Urban. Just what we need in a world that's forgotten that the simplest principles of success are still the most powerful ones."
—Robin Sharma, author of *The Monk Who Sold His Ferrari* and *The Greatness Guide*

Also by Hal Urban

Choices That Change Lives
Positive Words, Powerful Results
Life's Greatest Lessons

HAL URBAN

The **10** Commandments *of* Common Sense

WISDOM FROM THE SCRIPTURES FOR PEOPLE OF ALL BELIEFS

A FIRESIDE BOOK
PUBLISHED BY SIMON & SCHUSTER
New York   London   Toronto   Sydney

Fireside
A Division of Simon & Schuster, Inc.
1230 Avenue of the Americas
New York, NY 10020

First Fireside trade paperback edition August 2008

FIRESIDE and colophon are registered trademarks of Simon & Schuster, Inc.

For information about special discounts for bulk purchases,
please contact Simon & Schuster Special Sales at 1-800-456-6798
or business@simonandschuster.com.

Designed by Jan Pisciotta

Manufactured in the United States of America

10   9   8   7   6   5   4   3   2

The Library of Congress has cataloged the hardcover edition as follows:
Urban, Hal, 1940–   .
    The 10 commandments of common sense : wisdom
from the Scriptures for people of all beliefs / by Hal Urban.
        p.   cm.
    "A Fireside book."
    1. Spiritual life. 2. Conduct of life. I. Title.
    BL624 .U73 2007   205—dc22   2007001826

ISBN-13: 978-1-4165-3563-8
ISBN-10:   1-4165-3563-2
ISBN-13: 978-1-4165-3564-5 (pbk)
ISBN-10:   1-4165-3564-0 (pbk)

This book is dedicated to a man who doesn't need to read it. He knows the Scriptures intimately, and, more important, he puts them into practice every day.

TOM LICKONA

Thank you for the indescribable blessing you've been in this author's life—personally, professionally, spiritually.

Do not merely listen to the word, and so deceive yourselves.
Do what it says.

. . . Faith by itself, if it is not accompanied by action, is
dead.

—JAMES, 1:22, 2:17 NIV

Contents

PART II

FIVE THINGS THE SCRIPTURES TELL US TO DO
BECAUSE THEY'RE GOOD FOR US

Introduction

LIFE IS BETTER when we use common sense.

Unfortunately, it doesn't seem to be as common as it once was. Wise men and women have been teaching us the essential guidelines for living a good life for thousands of years, but we don't seem to be listening as much as we used to. They've been telling us to believe in something greater than ourselves, be kind, work hard, act with integrity, serve others, and open ourselves to the possibilities of wisdom and joy.

The problem is that we often get distracted and then stray from these essentials. We all have common sense, but we don't always use it. Instead of thinking for ourselves, we often let popular culture and the media do it for us. We allow ourselves to be persuaded by the steady barrage of ads and slick promotions that tell us the road to a happy life is paved with money, power, possessions, style, and fame. Uniting them all is the insidious notion that the more we focus on ourselves, the better life will be.

I spent about ten years living in that kind of make-believe world. Because of a shattering experience, I rejected my faith and everything pertaining to God. And both my values and my morals took a nosedive. I became the center of my own little universe. It was all supposed to lead to self-fulfillment. Sure enough, it did. I became full of myself. Ironically, I discovered that being full of myself actually led to the opposite: emptiness. And with it came unbearable pain.

When I admitted to myself that I couldn't cope with it any longer, I turned to a dear friend and mentor for advice. I chose him because he was older and wiser, and he seemed to have things figured out. He was a man of great inner peace and his life was full of joy. I wanted what he had, so I asked him to help me. He got right to the point.

"You need to return to your faith," he said simply. Then he added, "I'm not talking about just attending church and going through the motions but learning about your faith at a deeper and more personal level. I'm also talking about studying the Bible and applying its teachings to your life. They're not just for saints. They're for everybody because they're full of common sense, practical advice, and wisdom. I guarantee they'll work better than anything you've ever tried."

At that point I would have tried anything to ease the pain, so I followed his advice and returned to my faith. I did, indeed, learn about it in much greater depth, and, just as he said it would, it became far more personal and meaningful. He was also right about the Scriptures. They *are* full of common sense, practical advice, and wisdom. Studying them and applying them to my life really were more effective than anything I'd ever tried.

During the writing of my first three books, I often drew on the common sense and wisdom contained in the Scriptures. Each time I wrote I couldn't help thinking how nice it would be to know enough about the Bible to write an entire book based on its teachings. Then it finally dawned on me that I didn't need to be a biblical scholar. Mark Twain said, "Most people are bothered by those passages of Scripture they do not understand, but the passages that bother me are those I do understand." This is what I think he meant: the passages that speak directly to us, the ones that are easy to understand, also challenge us to become better human beings. They're hard to put into practice, but when we do, the rewards are beyond description. I think I understand enough about the Scriptures to know that they can change the direction and quality of a person's life. I wrote this book with the hope and prayer that they'll do for you what they've done for me. More specifically, I hope to do a few other things as well.

FOUR REASONS FOR WRITING THIS BOOK

1. Shed new light on the Scriptures for both believers and nonbelievers

The Bible means different things to different people. The Old Testament is the foundation of three major religions: Judaism, Christianity, and Islam. It contains history, poetry, proverbs, psalms, prayers, commandments, stories, and lessons in life. The New Testament is about the life of Jesus Christ and his teachings. In it, many references are made to the Old Testament, and it also contains prayers, commandments, stories, and lessons in life. Both the Old and New Testaments are the primary guidebooks for Christians throughout the world.

To believers, the Bible is the revealed Word of God, a sacred book that explains the ultimate truths about life. To nonbelievers, the Bible is often seen as a collection of well-intentioned writings, but not from God and often wrong. They also see it as the source of many problems and much divisiveness within our society. They often associate the Bible with the "religious Right," "born-agains," "evangelicals," flamboyant TV preachers, and those who loudly claim to be "saved" while condemning others.

The most difficult challenge in writing this book was trying to get both believers and nonbelievers to look at the Scriptures in a somewhat different light. It would have been much easier to write a book about the Scriptures solely for Christians. But that isn't my primary audience. I want to write for people of all beliefs. My primary concern about many people who claim to be Christians and claim the Bible as their guide is that either they're unfamiliar with some of its teachings or they choose to selectively ignore passages they find problematic or don't see as important enough to be applied to everyday life. I'm not trying to stereotype all Christians as hypocrites. I'm just saying that there often seems to be a disconnect between what many people say they *are* and what they *do*. It's my hope that this book will get those who claim to be Christians to look more closely at what the Scriptures are telling us and to be more consistent in putting its teachings into practice.

It's also the author's hope that nonbelievers will come to see the Scriptures differently. Instead of rejecting them simply because they're often associated with narrow-minded people with a particular religious or political agenda, I hope you'll be able to appreciate them for the wisdom, common sense, and sound advice they contain. You don't have to be a Buddhist or a Confucian to appreciate the wisdom and teachings of Buddha and Confucius (as I do), and you don't have to be a Christian to appreciate how much life can be enriched by the wisdom and teachings of Moses, David, Solomon, Jesus, Paul, John, and many others. The Bible contains an incredible array of universal principles that consistently help us understand life at a deeper level and live it more fully.

If you're unfamiliar with the Bible, I hope what you read here will pique your interest in learning more about it. It's not an easy book to understand. It requires hard work, diligence, a lot of patience, and help from others—the same things required to understand life. Some parts of it seem to jump out at us and are clearly and easily understood. Other parts are confusing and sometimes appear self-contradictory. Some of the teachings are easy to apply to daily life. And some seem impossible to apply for even a day. But like a giant puzzle, all the pieces eventually fit together. When they do, the picture becomes clearer, and if we apply what we learn, the quality of our lives is greatly enriched.

2. Show that the Bible is a valuable resource in mental health

Believers want essentially two things: a personal relationship with God and a meaningful and rewarding life. Nonbelievers want essentially one thing: a meaningful and rewarding life. The common denominator is that we all want to make the most of our lives, and in order to achieve this, we need to be mentally healthy. It's my contention that the Scriptures contain as good a prescription for mental health as any book ever written.

This is not a knock on psychology or psychologists. Their research, writing, and counsel are an invaluable resource and crucially important in helping us understand ourselves and some of the complexities of life. I would never tell someone who is clinically ill, "Read the Bible for the solution to your problems." It's not that simple, and it's not an either-or thing. Psychology and faith are not mutually exclusive. I've been the beneficiary of both psychological counseling and prescriptive books on the subject. Two that come to mind are *The Road Less Traveled* by the psychiatrist M. Scott Peck and *Man's Search for Meaning* by the psychiatrist Viktor Frankl, two of the best books I've ever read. I've also advised several people to seek professional counseling and have recommended numerous books written by Peck, Frankl, and others.

But the truth is, the Scriptures and prayer have enriched my life far beyond anything else I've ever experienced and far beyond anything I could have ever imagined.

As I explain in the account of my spiritual journey at the back of this book, I came to discover the richness of the Scriptures as the result of a long and painful journey in search of meaning. More than twenty-six years later, I'm still amazed at the simple yet powerful advice the Scriptures contain. The best thing about this advice is that it consistently works. Here's a good example:

> *A man's harvest in life will depend entirely on what he sows.*
>
> —GALATIANS 6:8 PHI*

This is one of those universal principles and a recurring theme in this book. Don't be surprised if you see this passage several more times—it's no mistake. Its meaning is simple: the

---

* See pages 17–18 for an explanation of the abbreviations used for the different versions of the Bible.

more good we think, the more good we have to say, and the more good we do, the more good will come back to us. What could be better for your overall well-being than that?

3. Propose another and more challenging 10 Commandments

Please understand that I'm not in any way suggesting that we ignore the original 10 Commandments or that we replace them with ten new ones. I really don't want to receive e-mails or letters that say, "Who do you think you are to suggest that you have a better idea than the authors of the Bible about the best way to live our lives?" Please hold off on that until you've read the next couple of paragraphs.

The original 10 Commandments are found in two places in the Old Testament: Exodus 20:1–17 and Deuteronomy 5:6–21. Most people, whether well versed in the Bible or not, are at least somewhat familiar with the "thou shalt nots" and the "thou shalts" of the 10 Commandments in the old King James translation. God gave them to Moses on two stone tablets (although Mel Brooks claims there were three), and Moses gave them to his people. They tell us things we should *never* do and things we should *always* do. The eight things we should *not* do are: honor other gods, worship false idols, misuse the name of God, murder, steal, commit adultery, give false testimony, and covet our neighbor's wife or goods. The two things we *should* do are honor our mothers and fathers and keep the Lord's day holy.

What I'm proposing here is that we continue to honor the original 10 Commandments. They're sacred. But I'm also proposing that we look more closely at some of the Bible's other "commandments." Many of them are far more challenging to put into practice than the ten written in stone. There are millions of decent people in the world who faithfully follow those rules of conduct every day. They don't need to reread the text to remind themselves what they should and should not be doing. Obviously, there are others who don't obey the original commandments. We do have murder, stealing, lying, adultery, and other wrongdoings in our society. But the percentage of people who do these things is relatively small.

If you'll look at the table of contents in this book, you'll see ten more commandments from both the Old and New Testaments: five things we should avoid doing because they can damage our lives and the lives of others, and five things we should devote ourselves to doing because they can enrich our lives and the lives of others. They're harder to put into practice than the original ten. I selected them because they all deal with everyday life and because putting them into action is challenging for most of us. These other 10 commandments provide wise and practical advice for all of us, no matter what we believe. That's the wonder of the Scriptures.

4. Continue a journey and thank my readers

In *Choices That Change Lives* I suggested that we should always be learning and be challenging ourselves to be better than we were the day before. I call it renewal. In that book I wrote about some very difficult tasks. Among them were to develop more humility, patience, and empathy, to learn to forgive, and to be more giving. All have been weak spots in my own life—

and I know I'm not alone. By reading extensively about each of them and then writing about them, I knew I'd have to work a lot harder at putting them into practice. I don't want to be one of those authors who writes one thing and does another. I'm not saying that I've mastered the ten lessons contained here, but I'm working harder on them than ever before, and I feel blessed with the wisdom and joy that result from the effort.

Readers often tell me that the common sense God blessed me with has helped them in a variety of ways under a variety of circumstances. They've asked me to continue writing, and I want to thank them for their powerful encouragement. So I'm at it again—working on a few more weak spots that trouble a great many of us.

I spend about a half hour each morning reading the Scriptures, with a particular focus on the Psalms, Proverbs, Ecclesiastes, and Isaiah in the Old Testament and all the Gospels and Epistles in the New Testament. When I ask myself how I'm doing at putting the Scriptures into practice on an everyday basis, the answer is always "Not nearly well enough." I need to work a lot harder at it, and I do so knowing the rewards: wisdom and joy—the ultimate prizes in this life. Maybe the same is true for you. If it is, I ask you to join me in this great challenge.

> *Lay hold of my words with all your heart; keep my commands and you will live.*
>
> *Get wisdom, get understanding; do not forget my words or swerve from them.*
>
> *Do not forsake wisdom, and she will protect you; love her, and she will watch over you.*
>
> —PROVERBS 4:4–6 NIV

THE AUTHOR'S FAITH AND HOW HE VIEWS THE BIBLE

When asked about my own faith, I answer that I'm a Christian. Shortly before I began writing this book, I was asked to explain my choice of faith and to define it, and I thought my answers would be useful to readers. Here's what I said.

"WHY ARE YOU A CHRISTIAN?"

I didn't hesitate to answer, "Because it works for me." And by that I meant that when I put the teachings of my faith into practice, the quality of my life is better and I make the quality of life of the people around me better. I'm more understanding, patient, and kind. I'm less selfish and more giving. I feel closer to God, I'm happier and at peace. In addition, it gives me hope. I believe in a life after this one and in a place called Heaven. The key phrase in the above paragraph is *when I put the teachings of my faith into practice.* That's the real challenge. I never do it as well as I'd like to. In fact of all the thousands of passages in the Bible the one that I personally relate to more than any other is this:

> *I do not understand what I do. For what I want to do I do not do, but what I hate I do.*
>
> —ROMANS 7:15 NIV

No one ever said it would be easy. The above was written about two thousand years ago by Saint Paul, one of the founders and great warriors of the early Christian Church. His faith was a challenge for him, as it was for great Jewish leaders like Moses and King David and later the Christian leader Saint Peter. They all had their flaws, which remind us that practicing one's faith is a challenge for everyone.

"WHAT KIND OF CHRISTIAN ARE YOU?"

To this I replied, "A thinking, open-minded, ecumenical, non-judgmental Christian." Here's what each of these terms means to me:

Thinking: God gave us a brain for a reason, and he wants us to use it everywhere, even in our places of worship. We don't honor God when we abandon our intellectual integrity. The Bible, like the U.S. Constitution, can be interpreted in different ways. It's our job to make every effort possible to understand how it speaks to us and how its teachings apply to our lives.

Open-minded: Life has a lot of complexities and mysteries that will never be completely understood here on Earth. I have a strong faith, but I don't make any claim to having all the answers, and it makes me uncomfortable when other people claim they do.

Ecumenical: I believe in friendly relations among different religions and in showing respect for belief systems other than my own. What others believe in their hearts is just as true to them as my beliefs are to me. I think we should look for common ground so we can use our faiths to make the world a better place.

Nonjudgmental: The Bible states clearly that we're not to judge others (see chapter 4), and I have real problems with people who do, especially in regard to matters of faith and who is and isn't "saved." I think we should all leave that to God and put our energy into honoring him by living according to the teachings of the Scriptures.

How We View the Bible

While I was writing this book, a Gallup poll was conducted nationwide (May 2006) to determine how Americans regard the Bible. Here's what it found:

28% believe that the Bible is the "actual Word of God and is to be taken literally."

53% believe that the Bible is the "inspired Word of God, but not everything in it should be taken literally."

19% believe that the Bible is an "ancient book of fables, legends, history, and moral precepts recorded by man."

Since I'm the author of a book based on teachings in the Scriptures, readers probably want to know which of these categories I fit into. I'm in the middle. I believe the Bible is inspired by God and written by men in order to teach us how to live effectively while we're here on Earth. When I read it, I look for the meaning in the message and then try to apply it to my life. For example, I don't take the story of creation and Adam and Eve in the Book of Genesis literally. However, I do take the meaning of this great story very seriously. Adam and Eve were booted from Paradise because of their pride, what many people call Original Sin. The nuns taught me at an early age that overcoming pride is a lifelong struggle and that it's the root of all our sins. I believed it then because the nuns told me. I believe it even more strongly now because I've lived for more than sixty years and have learned through experience that pride has tripped me up more times than I can count.

The point is that it doesn't matter which of the three categories you fit into or what faith you embrace. You can be a Buddhist monk, a rabbi, a Christian missionary, a Unitarian, an atheist, or anything else. No matter what we believe, we can all appreciate wisdom and common sense, no matter where it comes from. The Scriptures contain a lot of both.

Come now, let us reason together.
—ISAIAH 1:18 NIV

Author's Note on
Bible Terms and Translations

To make sure there's no misunderstanding, I want to clarify some of the key terms used in the title and within the text of this book. Further down you'll find a list of the translations of the Bible I referred to in writing this book.

Terms

Bible and Scriptures: These two terms are used interchangeably throughout the text. *Scripture* is sometimes interpreted as the sacred writings of all faiths, but in this book it is synonymous with the Bible, both the Old and New Testaments.

Commandment: Many people associate the word "command" with power, authority, and control. While it *can* be defined that way, it can also be synonymous with *instruction*, a much softer and more positive term. The teacher in me prefers this usage.

My understanding of "command" and "commandment" changed significantly after I started reading the Psalms, one of the most beautifully written books in the Scriptures. I

read parts of them every morning and agree with King
David that God's commands are full of his love for us and
were written to help us get on, and stay on, the right path.

> The law of the Lord is perfect, reviving the soul. The
> statutes of the Lord are trustworthy, making wise the
> simple.
>   The precepts of the Lord are right, giving joy to the
> heart.
>   The commands of the Lord are radiant, giving light to
> the eyes. . . .
>   By them is your servant warned; in keeping them there
> is great reward.
>
>   —PSALM 19:7–9, 11 NIV

Common sense: While not so common anymore, common sense is sound practical judgment that comes from experience rather than research. More than 75 percent of the
people who've reached out to me after reading one of my
books have thanked me for either the "practical wisdom" or
the "common sense" contained in them. I don't have a brilliant mind, but I do seem to have an orderly and logical
one, and its workings have produced books that apparently
appeal to nonintellectuals like me. I'm eternally grateful for
this, so I included "common sense" in the title in part to
thank and honor my readers.

Commonsense ideas are usually easy to understand. But
that doesn't mean they're easy to put into practice. A dear
friend of mine told me recently, "Common sense doesn't

assure a cakewalk." For instance, it's easy to understand the Golden Rule—"Treat other people exactly as you would like to be treated by them." (Matthew 7:12 PHI)—but it's far more challenging to put it into daily practice.

Man, men, he, his, him: Most books written before the 1970s did not use gender-inclusive language. It's something most of us try to do when writing or speaking. But the Bible was written thousands of years ago, and the old rules applied. I didn't want to alter the texts I drew from, so I hope you'll read all references to men as men *and* women. The Scriptures apply to all of us.

BIBLE TRANSLATIONS

The original Bible was written in the Greek and Hebrew languages. People who spoke other languages had to wait many years before they could read it in their native language. Fortunately, many dedicated biblical scholars have translated it for us. In fact, there are now more than fifty different translations of the Bible into English. I've used five of them. The first three listed below include both the Old and New Testaments. The last two are of the New Testament only. I've given each a three-letter abbreviation and have used them throughout the text so you will know which translation is being cited.

NIV: New International Version (Zondervan Corporation)

JER: The New Jerusalem Bible (Doubleday)

TLB: The Living Bible (Tyndale House)

PHI: The New Testament in Modern English by J. B. Phillips (Geoffrey Bles)

MES: The Message by Eugene H. Peterson (Navpress)

KJV: King James Version

One World, Many Beliefs

I HAVE GENUINE respect for what other people believe for several reasons. One is pure logic. Jews, Muslims, Hindus, Buddhists, and Christians all have different beliefs. And within each of these faiths there's a wide spectrum of beliefs. Who has the right to claim, "I practice the only true religion, and all the rest of you are wrong"? No one can prove scientifically and unequivocally that "my beliefs are the only correct ones, my way is the only way." When you can prove something, it's called science, not faith.

Yet faith is a powerful force in the lives of millions of people. It's the prism through which they view the world. It usually evolves from a combination of sources: culture, parents, friends, teachers, personal history, and books. Because we bring a different mix of these into the equation, we come to believe different things. And I think the world would be a much kinder place if we'd respect these differences among both believers and nonbelievers.

I taught many different subjects both in high school and at a university throughout my long teaching career, but the richest and most rewarding were the classes I taught on world religions. Religion is a fascinating subject, whether it's about history, people, beliefs, rituals, sacred texts, or traditions. The common thread seems to be most people's need to acknowledge that there's someone or something greater than us out there or up

there, whether you call that something Eternal Spirit, Life
Force, Higher Power, Jehovah, Yahweh, Allah, or God.

Studying religions, teaching about them, listening to my
students share their experiences, and reading the works of Huston Smith gave me a deep appreciation for what all people believe. Smith is one of the foremost authorities on the religions
of the world, and he's devoted his entire professional life to
studying them. We used his classic *The World's Religions* as the
textbook for the course.

Smith, a Christian, has not only researched the major religions of the world in depth, he's developed a great respect for
them. He says, "God reveals himself in all the major traditions
of the world."

> *What a strange fellowship this is, the God-seekers in every
> land, lifting their voices in the most disparate ways
> imaginable to the God of all life. . . . Does one faith carry
> the lead, or do the parts share in counterpoint and
> antiphony where not in full-throated chorus? We cannot
> know. All we can do is try to listen carefully and with full
> attention to each voice in turn as it addresses the divine.*
>
> —HUSTON SMITH

PART I

FIVE THINGS
THE SCRIPTURES
TEACH US TO AVOID

BECAUSE
THEY'RE BAD FOR US

AN IMPORTANT PART of living a good life is being able to avoid the things that are harmful to us. When we're small children, one of the first words we learn is "no." As in no, don't touch the stove because it will burn you; and no, don't run into the street because you might get run over. As we get older, we're told not to steal, fight, lie, cheat, use drugs, etc., because they're bad for us too. Then our doctors tell us to avoid smoking, drinking to excess, and eating too much for the simple reason that they can cause great harm to our health.

Long before our parents, teachers, and doctors started urging us to avoid those things, the Scriptures were written. Boiled down to the bare essentials, the Bible tells us to avoid doing what hurts our lives and to do what enriches our lives. Acting on all of them, including the don'ts, is ultimately positive. In fact, I count among my friends many people who celebrate *not* doing certain things. These include smoking, drinking, using drugs, overspending, and overeating. It's a victory for them and as worthy of celebration as a promotion or wedding.

The first part of this book explains five of the life-enhancing "no's" in the Bible. Actually, there are a lot more than five. I chose to focus on these essentials because they deal with issues that most people struggle with daily, issues that can lead to enormous damage to ourselves and to others if we're not paying attention.

Prologue
The Root of All Our Flaws

HERE ARE SIX of the ugliest words in the English language:

Selfish	Conceited	Self-centered
Egotistical	Haughty	Arrogant

Have you ever used any of these words to describe another person? If you have, they weren't exactly compliments, were they? Has anyone ever used one or more of them to describe you? Didn't make you feel too good, did it? These are harsh words, usually used to describe the type of person we dislike the most, the type of person we don't want to be, and the type of person we don't want our children to become. What causes people, including us, to behave in such nasty ways that we bring out these ugly words?

There's actually a simple answer. We're all born with a major flaw, and it leads to several others. Some people call it Original Sin. And many make a strong case that Original Sin is pride, described in one dictionary as "a haughty attitude shown by people who believe, often unjustifiably, that they are better than others." It was pride that caused the Archangel Lucifer to fall from grace, and it was pride that caused Adam and Eve to disobey God. It's our basic flaw and the root of most of our problems.

Pride is the first sin, the source of all other sins, and the worst sin.

—THOMAS AQUINAS

Although they're not in the Bible, most people are at least somewhat familiar with the Seven Deadly Sins. If you're not, or if you can't quite remember all of them, here they are:

Pride   Envy   Gluttony   Lust   Anger   Greed   Sloth

No matter where you find them, pride is always listed first. And if you take a close look at the others, you'll understand why. They're all offshoots of pride. They all involve some form of a "me first" approach to life.

Nearly all those evils in the world which people put down to selfishness are really far more the result of Pride. . . .

It is Pride that has been the chief cause of misery in every nation and family since the world began. . . .

The first step is to realize that one is proud. And a biggish step, too. At least, nothing whatever can be done before it. If you think you are not conceited, it means you are very conceited indeed.

—C. S. LEWIS

The above quotations may look familiar to you if you've read my most recent book, *Choices That Change Lives.* They're too good not to share again. As a teacher, I still rely on one of the most powerful tools available: reinforcement. Or as I learned in Latin class many years ago: *Repetitio mater studiorum est* (repetition is the mother of learning). The key point that the brilliant C. S. Lewis made is that we all have some degree of pride or conceit. We can't overcome it unless we first acknowledge it. It's one of those things the Scriptures tell us to avoid because it's bad for us. It can lead to all kinds of misery.

> *Pride goes before destruction, a haughty spirit before a fall.*
> —PROVERBS 16:18 JER

COMMANDMENT 1

DON'T BE SEDUCED BY POPULAR CULTURE

IT PREVENTS YOU FROM THINKING FOR YOURSELF

Old Testament Proverb

Leave your simple ways and you will live;
walk in the ways of understanding.

—PROVERBS 9:6 NIV

New Testament

Do not model your behavior on the contemporary world,
but let the renewing of your minds transform you.

—ROMANS 12:2 JER

COMMANDMENT 1

DON'T BE SEDUCED BY POPULAR CULTURE
IT PREVENTS YOU FROM THINKING FOR YOURSELF

> *Don't let the world around you squeeze you into its own mould.*
>
> —ROMANS 12:2 PHI

> *You are what you are because of what goes into your mind.*
>
> —ZIG ZIGLAR

TIMELESS ADVICE FROM THE WISEST PERSON EVER, BECAUSE SOME THINGS NEVER CHANGE

The wisdom of King Solomon is legendary, but few people other than those well versed in the Scriptures know the story behind it. It's told in chapter 3 of the First Book of Kings in the Old Testament. Solomon was only about twenty years old when he became king of Israel upon the death of his father, King David. He felt inadequate to the task and told God, "But I am only a little child and do not know how to carry out my duties." He asked for only one thing. It wasn't power or riches or long life. He asked instead for wisdom. God responded to him in a dream: "I will do what you have asked. I will give you a wise and discerning heart, so that there will never have been anyone like you, nor will there ever be."

> God gave Solomon wisdom and very great insight, and a breadth of understanding as measureless as the sand on the seashore.
>   Men of all the nations came to listen to Solomon's wisdom, sent by all the kings of the world, who had heard of his wisdom.
>
> I KINGS 3:29,34 NIV

During his reign of forty years, Solomon wanted to pass on his wisdom to both his contemporaries and future generations, so he put it into writing as the primary author of the Proverbs, Song of Songs, and Ecclesiastes. More than anything, he warns us to not be misled by others, particularly by "fools" and "sinners." In modern times those would be people who do stupid things and those who do illegal things. The truth is, there are times in our lives when we're swayed by both types. A word closely related to wisdom is discernment, or knowing how to make good choices, and Solomon repeatedly reminds us of this throughout his writings. Good choices don't happen naturally; we learn to make them with the help of wise people.

One of Solomon's urgent warnings is to not be enticed by the ways of the world. The dictionary tells us that to entice is to get a person to act in a particular way by offering something desirable. What were those desirable things in the tenth century B.C., when Solomon lived? He mentions money, possessions, power, and the opposite sex, and warns us to not be seduced by any of them. He also warns us against obtaining what we desire through dishonest means. Are things so much different in the twenty-first century A.D.? Not really, except perhaps that we seem to want more and more of it all. Some things never change, and Solomon's advice is as good today as it was three thousand years ago.

WHERE SCRIPTURES
AND ANTHROPOLOGY MEET

Don't become so well-adjusted to your culture that you fit into it without even thinking.

—ROMANS 12:2 MES

The natural act of thinking is greatly modified by culture; western man uses only a small fraction of his mental capabilities. . . . Man has put himself in his own zoo. He has so simplified his life and stereotyped his responses that he might as well be in a cage.

—EDWARD T. HALL,
PROFESSOR OF ANTHROPOLOGY

One of the most valuable and eye-opening subjects I ever studied in school was cultural anthropology. Somehow I missed it in high school and college, but in graduate school I became deeply immersed in it. In the early days of my doctoral studies in education, my adviser asked what my area of emphasis would be. I told her psychology. She then asked me how many courses I had taken in cultural anthropology. The answer was none. It seemed like a strange question. What did cultural anthropology have to do with human behavior? I soon found out that it has everything to do with human behavior. Together with sociology, it forms the foundation of psychology and leads us to a better understanding of what we do and why we do it.

Cultural anthropology, sometimes called social anthropology, is the study of human behavior as influenced by other people and culture. As much as we'd like to think of ourselves as individuals and independent thinkers, the truth is that we're often not either. From infancy on we unwittingly go through a process anthropologists call enculturation. In other words, we become products of our culture. The way we dress, the way we talk, the music and entertainment we enjoy, the products we buy, the food we eat, the beliefs and values we hold dear are all closely connected to our culture. It's impossible to be free of the influence of culture, but we can become aware of it and resist its seduction.

Let me use an embarrassing example from my own life to demonstrate the influence of popular culture. I was in my mid-thirties when I started studying cultural anthropology. Since education is supposed to increase our understanding of the world and our self-awareness, I had to ask myself if popular culture had influenced a think-for-yourself guy like me. The honest and humbling answer was yes—in a big way. When I took a good look, I realized that popular culture had played an enormous role in my life. I had this moment of self-awareness in the 1970s, a decade many of us would like to forget.

I cringe when I see pictures of myself taken during that period. I had long hair, a big mustache, and muttonchop side-burns. I wore bell-bottom pants and flowery shirts with big collars. I was into everything pop psychology had to offer because my goal was to be "self-actualized." In addition to my impressive command of psychobabble, I used terms like "groovy" and "far out." And yes, I listened to disco music, including the Bee Gees. But the worst part of all was that I thought I was pretty cool.

How do things like this happen, even to educated people? It's simple. Popular culture is one of the most powerful and seductive forces in our lives. We're bombarded daily with shallow messages about what we should look like and all the things we should own, because then we'll be cool. If we allow popular culture to take over, as I did, we cease to think for ourselves. And we deny ourselves the opportunity to become the type of people we could be. That's why Solomon told us to "Put away foolishness" and Jesus told us, "You must change your hearts."

It is only with the heart that one sees rightly.
—ANTOINE DE SAINT-EXUPÉRY

LIFE IS AN EXERCISE IN MINDLESS CONFORMITY

Don't copy the behavior and customs of this world, but be a new and different person with a fresh newness in all you do and think.

—ROMANS 12:2 TLB

During the last several years of my teaching career I used the heading above to launch into an exercise I used with both my high school and university students. I wrote those words on the board and gave each student a half sheet of paper with the following instructions: "At the top of your paper, write the word 'agree' or 'disagree' in regard to your feelings about this statement. It has to be one or the other. Then in one concise paragraph, explain why."

This simple assignment quickly became one of my favorites because it consistently produced two wonderful results: first, it always got my students to think; and second, it never failed to provoke a lively discussion, which often included some healthy disagreement. Ironically, more than three-fourths of the high school kids answered "disagree" (is there a period in our lives when fitting in is *more* important than it is during adolescence?), while more than three-fourths of the adults answered "agree." Those results surprised me the first time, but not afterward. Kids, especially teenagers, feel an enormous amount of peer pressure to conform. They do exactly that but don't seem to be aware of it. Even if they are, they rarely admit it. Adults, who feel much less peer pressure, are simply more aware that we often do things to conform without thinking first, and it's usually what everyone else is doing.

The conversation in both age groups always led to the topic of how we make choices. My main contribution to this part of the discussion was always the same: "If we don't learn to consciously make our own choices, either we'll make choices unconsciously (not even aware that we're choosing to do one thing over another) or we'll let other people make them for us." One year a very bright high school senior said he agreed with me and then asked, "But how do you *learn* to make conscious and independent choices?" An excellent question. I said we learn to make our own choices only after we become aware of all the powerful influences in our culture.

To make my point, I told him and the rest of the class about what I was like in the 1970s. They laughed, and some even asked if I had any old yearbooks so they could see pictures. I said I'd burned them. In spite of my college education and thirty years of life experience, I'd been leading a life of "mindless conformity." I also explained a little about cultural anthropology and sociology and why I thought they should be required courses beginning in junior high school.

This topic seemed to genuinely intrigue both my teenage and adult students. The first time we did this exercise, another good question came up, namely, "What aspects of our culture do you think most influence the choices we make?" I surmised aloud that we would get different answers from different people, so I suggested that we answer it collectively. The students gave me their answers, and I wrote them on the board. Over the years, there was remarkable consensus. These are what they saw (in no particular order) as the most powerful influences in our culture:

Advertising	Peers	Family	Television
Education	Faith	Magazines	Celebrities
Fashion	Fads	Books	Tradition
Politics	Race	Work	Money

Although we devoted only one class to the cultural influences that affect our choices, it *did* have an enormous and lasting impact on many of my students. At the end of each semester I taught, there was a final exam. Part of that exam was of the take-home variety, and it had only one question: "What are the three most valuable things you learned in this class? Give a reason for each." Our discussion about "mindless conformity" and the influence of popular culture on decision making was one of the three on more than 80 percent of the papers. One of my adult students summed it up the best: "Wow! What an eye-opener! *Culture* was just another word to me before we did this. Now I'm constantly aware of its influence. Life *can* be an 'exercise in mindless conformity,' but not if we learn to make our own choices."

> *We must make the choices that enable us to fulfill the deepest capacities of our real selves.*
>
> —THOMAS MERTON

> *How much better to get wisdom than gold, to choose understanding rather than silver.*
>
> —PROVERBS 16:16 NIV

CELEBRITIES AND HEROES

> *No country in the world is so driven by personality, has such a hunger to identify with personalities, larger-than-life personalities especially, as this one.*
>
> —PETER JENNINGS

Entertainment is a critically important aspect of life. Without it we'd work too hard and too long, take ourselves too seriously, get bored, get on one another's nerves, and probably crack due to an overload of stress. We need a release, and, next to physical exercise, entertainment is the best way to get it. Fortunately, there's no shortage of people to provide it for us—talented actors, athletes, dancers, comedians, writers, etc. Many of them are so talented they become famous. We call them celebrities and sometimes superstars, pop idols, or icons.

What these talented people do in their professional lives is both important and wonderful. But is what they do in their private lives equally important and wonderful? Why is there such a national obsession with celebrities? Why do we need to know whom they're dating, with whom they're cheating, whose babies they're having, why they split up, where they're vacationing, what they're wearing, what they eat and drink, and where? Why is there an entire industry built on what the stars are doing?

It's because millions of people want to know these things and are willing to pay for the information. The industry rakes in billions of dollars every year. Just take a look at what publications are selling at the supermarket checkout.

Here are a few examples of the influence celebrities wield in this country:

- Journalists are paid large salaries just to write gossip about the stars.

- Tabloids and other publications dealing with celebrities are among the best sellers.

- Thousands of babies born in this country each year are named after celebrities.

- People spend billions of dollars on products endorsed by celebrities.

- Biographies and autobiographies of celebrities consistently appear on the best-seller lists.

- There are thousands of fan clubs and memorabilia collectors devoted to the stars.

- Celebrities have gained enormous influence in our government by endorsing political candidates or by running for office themselves. (The Governator wasn't the first—remember Ronald Reagan?)

- There are several TV programs devoted entirely to the private lives of the stars.

- Most major Internet portals have a prominent section we can click on to get all the latest dirt on the people who entertain us.

- The private lives of entertainers are the topic of conversation among millions of people every day. They're talked about as if they were close friends or family members. This is the scariest of all.

Psychologists and sociologists tell us this is happening because so many people lack an identity of their own. They feel unfulfilled. To fill the void, they attach themselves to someone famous and live vicariously through that person. How incredibly sad this is. It's also sad that celebrities have so much influence in shaping our culture, because the private lives of many of them are less than admirable. Still, they have an enormous amount of power in regard to our society's trends and values. And since the media can't seem to get enough of them, we're bombarded daily from all sides with information about the "lives of the stars."

Of particular concern is how much influence celebrities have in our children's lives. Having been in close contact with kids for more than forty years, I've experienced it firsthand. It's truly frightening how susceptible young minds are to the things going on in pop culture. This was one of the main reasons for doing the "exercise in mindless conformity" activity.

Another activity I did with my students prompted them to think about the people who influence them the most, and how. I've done this activity hundreds of times, both in my own classroom and in schools and colleges across the country. I always begin with this question: "Who are your heroes?" Whether I'm speaking to thirty kids in my own classroom or in a packed auditorium on the other side of the country, I ask them to write down their answers. When they're finished writing, I ask them to tell us who their heroes are. There are a few exceptions, but an overwhelming majority of the students (including graduate students in college), give me the names of celebrities.

Then comes another question: "Are you confusing the word 'celebrity' with the word 'hero'?" That usually results in a lot of

blank stares and a few "huh?"s. I explain that there's a big difference between the two. A celebrity is a famous person; a hero is
someone we know and admire, a person we want to emulate, a
role model. We do the exercise again. The answers the second
time are usually parents, grandparents, older brothers and sisters, teachers, coaches, pastors, and a few others. There's a big
difference between a celebrity and a hero.

That part of the exercise is followed by real-life stories.
Most kids (and adults) will tune out a lecture, but they'll listen
to a good story. I tell them about the influence some of my heroes have had in helping me become a better and happier person. Those heroes include my mom, teachers I was lucky
enough to have in both high school and college, a college class-
mate who had polio, a basketball coach, a fellow teacher, and a
colleague in the character education movement. I urge students to look around. There are genuine heroes in their midst,
and there will be more in the future. And I urge them to pay
more attention to their heroes and less attention to celebrities.

These are the types of people Solomon was referring to
when he advised us to learn from those who can influence our
lives in positive ways. Instead of being seduced by celebrities
and popular culture, we need to learn to think for ourselves.
We also need to understand that thinking *for* ourselves doesn't
necessarily mean thinking *by* ourselves. There are plenty of
people around who can serve as our mentors and help us make
good choices. Solomon repeatedly tells us to "Get wisdom, get
understanding." He also tells us, "Do not forsake wisdom, and
she will protect you; love her and she will watch over you"
(Proverbs 4:5–6 NIV). And then he tells us how we can attain
this wisdom:

He who walks with the wise grows wise.

—Proverbs 13:20 NIV

How Are You Spending Your Time?

We must decide what is really important, really necessary, make it a priority, and make time. Otherwise the siren call of the world will always keep us busy and distracted from what really is important. What really counts?

—Matthew Kelly

In the 1970s, time management became all the rage among businessmen and -women, students, parents, pastors, teachers, service providers, and just about everyone else. Alan Lakein had come out with his best-selling book *How to Get Control of Your Time and Your Life* in 1973, and suddenly we all needed to learn to manage our time more effectively. To most people caught up in the craze, time management meant getting more done in less time. And since everyone knows that "time is money," they concluded that mastering their time would increase their net worth.

Unfortunately, one of the most important aspects of successful time management was completely missed. That aspect is *priorities*! In chapter 9 of his book Lakein advises his readers to "Set priorities, set priorities, set priorities." Four chapters later, he asks what he considers the most important question in the book: "What is the best use of my time right now?" Somehow, this central theme in Lakein's message was bypassed.

Like most other people who got sucked into this craze, I had to learn to manage my time more efficiently, so I signed up for a seminar. I was lucky. The time efficiency expert who taught it started with these words: "Everything I'm going to teach you is about priorities. The sole purpose of this seminar is to get you to examine your values, establish your priorities, and help you do a better job of living by them."

He started with a simple yet powerful exercise. He handed us a sheet of lined paper that had two column headings near the top. On the left was **Priorities,** and on the right was **Time.** In the first column we were asked to list the five things most important to us, in order of importance. In the second column we were asked to write the five things that occupied most of our time while awake, in order of time spent. It was an eye-opener for most of us attending, because we found a disconnect between what we were saying was important and how we were spending our time.

The two words the seminar leader used the most were "priorities" and "balance." He said most of us don't live according to our priorities because, first, we never take the time to establish them in writing; and second, because we get seduced by popular culture to the point of letting it dictate the way we live, the way we spend our time. That makes balanced living impossible. He said the people who are most effective in managing their time and their lives not only establish their priorities but make sure enough time is blocked out for them.

A brilliant book about living according to our priorities came out in 1994. It's called *First Things First,* written by Stephen R. Covey, A. Roger Merrill, and Rebecca R. Merrill. In the introduction to the book they ask these three penetrating questions:

1. "If you were to pause and think seriously about the 'first things' in your life—the three or four things that matter most—what would they be?"

2. "Are these things receiving the care, emphasis, and time you really want to give them?"

3. "Why is it that so often our first things aren't first?"

In the next 306 pages the authors help their readers answer these and many other important questions about priorities, time, balance, principles, and service to others. They warn that their message is not an easy one: "It may not be popular in a quick-fix, short-term, consumption-based world." And they conclude the book by challenging us to look beyond the enticements of our culture and ask ourselves this question: "Is there something I feel I could do to make a difference?"

There are things all of us can do to make better use of our time. The first step is not allowing ourselves to be seduced by popular culture.

There is a time for everything, and a season for every activity under heaven.

—ECCLESIASTES 3:1 NIV

Make the best use of your time, despite all the difficulties of these days.

—EPHESIANS 5:16 PHI

COMMANDMENT 2

DON'T FALL IN LOVE WITH MONEY AND POSSESSIONS
IT WILL MAKE YOU GREEDY AND SHALLOW

Old Testament Proverbs

Whoever trusts in riches will fall.

—PROVERBS 11:28 NIV

A greedy man brings trouble to his family.

—PROVERBS 15:27 NIV

New Testament

For the love of money is a root of all kinds of evil.

—TIMOTHY 6:10 NIV

For a man's real life in no way depends upon the number of his possessions.

— LUKE 12:15 PHI

COMMANDMENT 2

DON'T FALL IN LOVE WITH MONEY AND POSSESSIONS
IT WILL MAKE YOU GREEDY AND SHALLOW

*For wherever your treasure is, you may be certain that
your heart will be there too!*

—MATTHEW 6:21 PHI

MONEY—THE GREAT AMERICAN OBSESSION

*Too many of us look upon Americans as dollar chasers.
This is a cruel libel, even if it is reiterated thoughtlessly by
the Americans themselves.*

—ALBERT EINSTEIN

There are few things in life more fascinating—and at times
more depressing—than the American obsession with money.
It's fascinating when people use their creativity and their passion to develop something that improves the quality of our
lives and they become wealthy in the process, as the creators of
Google have. They've helped map the vast ocean of information available to us on the Internet and gotten rich enough to

buy other billion-dollar companies in the process. Good for them. On the other hand, it's downright depressing to see other people lose themselves in the pursuit of the almighty dollar. They risk their health, damage their relationships, and end up miserable. If they use illegal means to try to acquire wealth, they may even find their way to prison.

Fueling the drive for riches is our society, one that glorifies the rich and the famous. The all-encompassing media can't get enough of them. So from the time we're old enough to think, we're barraged by messages telling us that success and having a lot of money are synonymous. I used a sentence completion exercise with both my high school and adult students that demonstrates my point. One sentence began, "Success is . . ." More than 90 percent of the responses contained the words "money," "wealth," or "rich." It's part of the enculturation process referred to earlier. It's also a major part of how we can be seduced by popular culture (see chapter 1).

In the subtitle of this chapter I used two strong words, "greedy" and "shallow," to describe the effects of this seduction. We get greedy when we start thinking that our worth as humans is determined by the amount of money and possessions we have. No matter how much we have, we strive for more because having more means we're more worthy. And we become shallow when we start thinking more about money and the things it will buy than we do about family, friendship, learning, achievement, personal growth, and service to others. There's nothing wrong with earning a living to support yourself and your family; but it's those other things that give our lives meaning and make us truly rich.

I can imagine someone reading this and thinking, "It's easy

for you to talk about not needing to get rich because you're *already* rich." I've heard that comment a few times when I give a talk called "The Real Meaning of Success." It might be helpful if I briefly explain both my financial history and my philosophy of money.

A 58-Year Struggle to Make Ends Meet

The Lord sends poverty and wealth; he humbles and he exalts.
—1 Samuel 2:7 NIV

I was born into what would today be called a lower-middle-class family. My father, a ninth-grade dropout, was an iron-worker, and my mother stayed home to tend to my brother and me. We never knew poverty simply because my dad wouldn't let that happen. But we did know hard times. When my dad was seriously injured on the job, we had to live on his disability pay for about a year. We went without a lot of things when he was working full-time, and we went without even more while he was injured. He left ironwork for a while to drive a logging truck and worked long hours to provide for us. In fact, he worked so many hours that he eventually became ill, which meant more time on disability.

Looking back on those days, the most valuable thing I learned was how to spend money sensibly. My mom and dad never did anything foolish with their money. They didn't spend more than they took in, and they didn't pile up debt. When there was less money coming in, we went without. My mom went to work when I was in the seventh grade so they could save money to put me through college, as I was the first in my family to have that ambition. They were probably happier than I was when the University of San Francisco, a private school, offered me a basketball scholarship. I got a "full ride"— it covered room and board, tuition, fees, and books for four years. It seemed like a godsend to my family.

I got married shortly after graduating from college and worked my way through grad school for the next two years. Our first son, Dan, was born while I was working on my teaching credentials, and a year later Mark was born while I was working on my master's degree. Besides being a full-time graduate student, I taught one evening and one day class at the university and worked thirty-five hours a week as a recreation director. Somehow we managed to survive those two years, but not without a student loan.

In the fall of 1966 I began my career in a low-paying profession: teaching. My yearly salary in that first year was $8,400. I had seriously considered becoming a lawyer—better pay and more prestige—but decided that it was more important to do what I loved every day than it was to make a lot of money. Sure, I wanted to provide for my family, but I can honestly say that being rich was never an ambition. Shortly after I began my teaching career our third son, Mike, was born, and though we lived frugally, my meager income would not pay all the bills. To supplement my four-figure salary, I taught one night at the university (as well as summer sessions) and another night at the local community college. Vacation wasn't a word I had occasion to use, unless the subject was someone else's trip.

When Mike was two, my wife informed me that being married to a struggling teacher was not her idea of the good life, and she filed for divorce. Although she took the three boys with her, I gained full custody of them a short time later. If you're a parent, I don't need to tell you they came with a slew of financial responsibilities—such as the costs of nursery school and child care, all of which further strained my income. Fortunately, my mother, who lived thirty miles away, often came to the rescue. She stayed with my sons while I taught at night, helped out with some of the housekeeping and laundry, and bought the kids a lot of clothes. We couldn't have made it without her.

That was the state of affairs for ten years. It seemed as though I was forever finding my wallet and bank account empty, especially at the end of each month. Our sole means of transportation during those years was a used Volkswagen bus I'd bought from a fellow teacher. As my parents and I had done many years earlier, my sons and I went without a lot of things. But despite the struggle, we still lived a good life, appreciated what we *did* have, laughed a lot, and came to understand that the best things in life really don't cost a cent.

Things improved financially when I married Cathy. While I didn't marry her for her money, the fact that she had a job and a monthly income helped ease the strain. After eighteen years, I was finally able to skip the summer teaching session and go on a low-budget vacation. Of course, college expenses were right around the corner. There was one year when all three were at the university at the same time. Somehow we managed, and Mike graduated when I was approaching the age of fifty. Right afterward I had my first experience with something I'd only read about in the business section: disposable income! It took a while to get used to it.

When I was fifty-eight, my first book, which was then self-published, took off, and suddenly I had two streams of income. At the same time, my speaking career, which had started somewhat by accident at age fifty-five, also gained steam—additional unexpected income. What in the world was going on here? What was I supposed to do with all this extra money? The answer came in part from my parents' example: be smart with it; shut out popular culture's mantra of spend, spend, spend. Instead I would do good things with it. And, most important, be thankful for it.

Earn Honestly, Spend Wisely

I know how to live when things are difficult and I know how to live when things are prosperous.

—Philippians 4:12 PHI

Because of my upbringing and lifelong commitment to a low-paying profession, I've always taken a commonsense approach to money. I look upon it as both a necessity and a resource. We need money to pay for our most basic physical needs, and beyond that we can use it to do good things for ourselves, our families, worthy causes, and people in need. When I wrote *Life's Greatest Lessons* in 1990, long before I had anything more than my teacher's salary to live on, I addressed the money issue first. I called chapter 1 "Success Is More Than Making Money." I believed that before I had any extra money, and I believe it now. It isn't how much money you make; it's what you do with your life that counts.

I'll repeat a few lines from that first chapter: "There's nothing wrong with money. There's nothing wrong with wanting it, and there's nothing wrong with having it, even in large amounts. Honestly acquired and well spent, it can be a resource for much good. . . . There's nothing illegal or immoral about being rich, but it isn't everything." Whether we're rich or poor financially, what really matters is how much we learn, how hard we work, what we achieve, how we treat others, how much integrity we have, and what we do to make the world a better place.

As indicated in the heading above, my philosophy of money is to earn it honestly and spend it wisely. There'll be more about earning it honestly in chapter 8, so at this point I want to offer a simple formula for spending wisely. There are many passages in both the Old and New Testaments that advise us to be good stewards of our money. In other words, we need to manage it well. Sadly, many people in this country manage their money matters very poorly indeed. If you're one who struggles with this issue, let me offer two simple suggestions. They're based on logic, common sense, and sound biblical advice:

1. Write down your financial priorities in order of necessity, and then spend accordingly. For all of us, necessity number one is paying for our physical needs—housing, food, clothing, and medical care. Spend what's left, if there is any, on the things that matter the most to you. We all have different needs. If you're one of those fortunate people who brings in more than you need, establish a second list of priorities for how that extra money will be spent. My list includes family, savings, church, charity, home, education (including books), and travel. Again,

your list is going to look different from mine and from the list your brother, sister, or neighbors would write.

2. Get help if you need it. There are several good books available that give practical advice about how best to handle one's finances. One is *Personal Finance for Dummies* by Eric Tyson. I also recommend talking to people who are knowledgeable in this field. It could be a professional financial counselor (consider a "fee only" planner; in other words, someone who doesn't earn a commission for selling you insurance or mutual funds) or someone you know personally who could serve as a financial mentor. The idea is the same as above: make a specific, written plan, and stick with it.

When Money and Possessions Become Problems: Worshiping False Idols and Coveting What Others Have

You may worship no other god but me.
You shall not make yourselves any idols . . .
You must never bow or worship it in any way. . . .

—Commandments 1 and 2
Exodus 20:3–5 TLB

You shall not covet your neighbour's house . . . or anything
that belongs to your neighbor.

—Commandment 10
Exodus 20:17 NIV

When I was in elementary school, I learned and memorized the 10 Commandments. You probably remember things you memorized as a child too. I remember the First Commandment as "I am the Lord thy God. Thou shalt not have false gods before me," or, as the Jerusalem Bible states, "You shall have no other gods to rival me" (Exodus 20:3). I can't remember if I was in the third or fourth grade when we learned the 10 Commandments, but I do remember that this first one stumped quite a few of us. We understood the concept of God, but what the heck was a "false god"? Our teachers explained that some people in those days worshiped things other than God. Among them were mountains, animals, and statues. They were often called idols. Essentially, God said to Moses, "No more idols."

At our tender age we couldn't understand why people would want to worship anyone but God. Our teacher explained that even in modern times many people continue to worship idols. We lived within view of Mount Shasta, so we figured maybe some people worshiped that. The only famous statue we knew was the Statue of Liberty, so we put that on the list too. The animal was a little harder to figure, but we came up with the lion because he was the "king of beasts." Our teacher got a chuckle out of our conclusions, but she had other idols in mind. Basically, there were only two: money and things.

We learned the Tenth Commandment as "Thou shalt not covet thy neighbor's goods." More confusion. What does "covet" mean, and what are "goods?" We were told that "covet" meant to desire something that someone else had and that it was wrong because it led to all kinds of problems. We also learned that "goods" was just another word for "things." That seemed kind of funny to us, so for the next few days we went around saying things like "Thou shalt not covet my goods, especially my Hershey bar."

But we got the main two points: no worshiping false idols and no coveting things. Of course, people still do both. Here are a few recent examples.

WORSHIPING MONEY

In 1998 I was invited to attend a three-day seminar on the importance of establishing our priorities and bringing balance to our lives. Most of the attendees were wealthy people in the business world—executives in insurance, banking, real estate, investment counseling, corporations, and so on. I felt a bit out of place being the only classroom teacher and low-income person there. One of the first activities was to share our most important goal in a small-group setting. The guy who led off was only thirty-eight and the youngest person at the seminar. He was nice-looking, neatly dressed, and a bit intense. "My number one goal is forty before forty!" I felt even more out of place; he was apparently using some form of lingo from the business world that everyone in the group understood except me. And as it turned out, most of them *did* know what he meant.

Sounding like the guy who just fell off the turnip truck, I had to ask him to explain. He looked at me somewhat incredulously and said even more emphatically, "I want to have forty million dollars in my portfolio before I turn forty." Then he added, "I only have about four or five million more to go." I was so surprised I didn't know what to say, but I remember thinking that I lived on another planet. One of the other guys in the group high-fived him; several smiled knowingly. One raised a fist, shook it, and said, *"Yeah!"*

I couldn't help wondering why, when you had $35 or $36 million, you'd need another cent. But I didn't dare ask the question out loud. Since we were there to examine our priorities and ways to bring more balance to our lives, I innocently asked, "What about your family?" Wrong question. Visibly upset, he fired back, "Who do you think I'm doing this for?" This was not getting off to a good start, and, as graciously as I could, I smiled and nodded my head as though I understood and motioned for the next person to share his goal. I wasn't convinced that Mr. 40-40 was doing it for his family, and, based on that and several other things he said in the next few days, I could only conclude that he had missed out on the lessons I had gotten about worshiping idols.

WORSHIPING POSSESSIONS

Mr. 40-40 reminded me of another recent encounter with a false god. One of my friends was making a presentation at a conference of businesspeople in San Francisco and asked me to attend. I was introduced to several people throughout the day, and during one of the breaks I found myself in a small, excited group. They were all congratulating a man I'll call Stan, and he was absolutely beaming. I heard him say, "This is my first one, and this is the proudest day of my life. I've waited a long time for it." He was also in his late thirties, and I had to assume that his wife had just given birth to their first child. Remembering how happy I was when my first child was born, I also congratulated him and asked him if he had any pictures yet. He triumphantly said, "Yes!" and pulled a photo out of a folder. He handed it to me and said, "This is my baby. Isn't she beautiful?" It was a picture of a Mercedes-Benz. The other people in the group absolutely gushed over it. It had never occurred to me to carry around a picture of my Volkswagen bus before, but at that moment I sure wished I'd had one.

Stan the Mercedes Man followed up with something that made the whole thing seem even more surreal: "I can't really afford it, but when people see me drive by they're going to say, 'There goes a guy who's *made* it.'" As it turned out, most of the conversations I heard that day revolved around money, cars, vacations in exotic places, jewelry, and other luxury items. And once again, I felt like an alien. In fact, when people asked me what I did and I told them I was a high school teacher, they were immediately, clearly uncomfortable. They didn't know what to say. A few did manage to come up with an awkward "Oh, that's nice."

Such situations are not uncommon. My guess is that you're recalling a similar experience yourself right now. We witness these scenes unfolding, we hear or overhear conversations, we read about them on a daily basis, and they remind us anew about the enormous power of popular culture to seduce us into thinking that we'd be happy and fulfilled if only we had a lot of money and a lot more things than we have right now. Life becomes distorted when we worship idols. Not only do we miss out on the real joys of life, we often cause great pain to both ourselves and others.

Make money your god and it will plague you like the devil.
                                        —HENRY FIELDING

HOW MUCH IS ENOUGH?

*Whoever loves money never has enough; whoever loves
wealth is never satisfied with his income.*
                                        —ECCLESIASTES 5:10 NIV

We all suffer from the same disease. It's called "more."
                                        —WAYNE DYER

Do you think Mr. 40-40 was satisfied when he reached his
magic number? Was $40 million enough? Or do you think he's
now Mr. 50-50? Can he answer the question at the top of this
section? More important, can *you* answer it? Have you ever
tried? It's the single most difficult question to answer regarding
money, and very few ever have, whether they're poor, middle-
class, or wealthy. Yet it's the key to peace of mind regarding
matters pertaining to money.

    In the 1970s, when I was struggling and doing a lot of
moonlighting in order to pay the bills, a mentor gave me some
of the best financial advice of my life. He was a wealthy man
who had known hard times growing up and for most of his
early adulthood. He said that being able to answer the question
"How much is enough?" was critically important and that his
own mentor had asked it of him several years earlier. He ad-

vised me to sit down with paper and pencil and add up all my
regular monthly expenses. They were mortgage, utilities, gro-
ceries, clothing, gas, insurance, and the dreaded "unexpected,"
which managed to raise its ugly head every month. We added
it up, and he said that was how much was *enough*. He said, "Be
thankful if you can take care of your family's needs every
month because a lot of people can't, and a lot of others live in
poverty." He said that anything left over (a rarity in those days)
was "discretionary" money. He advised me to save whenever I
could, to invest wisely when possible, and to provide my family with a special treat whenever I could.

His definition of "enough," along with his reminder to be
thankful, proved to be invaluable. Somehow, this wise man
both simplified and crystallized the whole money issue, and
I've followed his advice for more than thirty years. When I
didn't have much, I was still thankful for being able to take
care of my family's basic needs. That *was* enough. He also
gave me some good advice regarding discretionary money, although at the time I didn't think I'd ever have any. He said,
"If you ever find yourself with more than you need, be thankful for that also. Treat yourself once in a while, and put the
rest where it can help other people." He finished our little
mentoring session with a one-sentence warning: "Wanting
too much is what gets people into trouble." Then he shared
three passages from the Scriptures that had guided his own
handling of money:

> For what good is it for a man to gain the whole world at the
> price of his own soul?
>
> —MATTHEW 16:26 PHI

*Keep your lives free from the lust for money: Be content
with what you have.*

—Hebrews 13:5 PHI

*Do not store up for yourselves treasures on earth . . .
But store up for yourselves treasures in heaven.*

—Matthew 6:19 NIV

A Nation of Debtors

*Understanding is a fountain of life to those who have it,
but folly brings punishment to fools.*

—Proverbs 16:22 NIV

*Do not wear yourself out to get rich; have the wisdom to
show restraint.*

—Proverbs 23:4 NIV

*The rich lords it over the poor, the borrower is the lender's
slave.*

—Proverbs 22:7 JER

Throughout the Proverbs, Solomon both warns and advises us.
He warns us not to be enticed by the ways of the world, especially when it comes to money and possessions. And he constantly reminds us, as he does in the first of the three passages
above, that when we do foolish things, we'll eventually pay for
them. He advises us to show restraint when it comes to matters

of money and tells us that too much borrowing enslaves us to the lenders. Keep in mind that this was thousands of years before the invention of plastic money (credit cards). Later, in Ecclesiastes, he looks back on the many things he acquired during his lifetime, and he calls them meaningless.

Solomon was no stranger to wealth (he was a king, after all) but even he would be astounded at what's going on today. In 2003, CNN, in conjunction with *Money* magazine, posted an article on its Web site under the headline "Spending Our Way to Disaster." In the opening sentence, Justin Lambert, the CNN/*Money* senior writer, wrote, "The American consumer has become deeply addicted to spending, running up ever higher levels of debt in order to live in a fashion that is beyond his means. And the world has become equally addicted to the consumer continuing to burn through cash." Three thousand years ago Solomon wrote, "As goods increase, so do those who consume them" (Ecclesiastes 5:11 NIV), so maybe he wouldn't be surprised at the average American's personal finances after all.

In April 2006, American Consumer Credit Counseling published the following statistics:

- The lending industry has deemed 78 percent of American households to be creditworthy.

- The personal credit card debt carried by the average American is $8,562.

- The average American couple pays more than $2,000 per year in interest on credit cards.

- The average American consumer has eight credit cards.

- More than 20 percent of all credit cards in the United States are maxed out.

- More than 1.3 million credit card holders declared bankruptcy in 2005.

- Personal bankruptcies in the United States doubled between 1995 and 2005.

- More than 40 percent of United States families spend more than they earn.

I know these numbers are real, but it still amazes me that so many people spend money they don't have. They carry huge credit card debt, take out home equity and car loans, and end up living from month to month in a financial sinkhole. Why is this happening on such a large scale? And why has it been on the increase since the 1980s? Historians, sociologists, and economists all agree that five major trends have helped fuel our debt-crazed society. It's easy to see how they feed off one another:

1. The explosion in technology has made all forms of media more accessible to more people—and the media wield greater influence than ever before. The more media-savvy (read younger) you are, the more likely you're the target of the seductive messages of pop culture.

2. Technology itself is seductive. There are far more gadgets—from camera phones to iPods to all the accessories that go with them—that people simply feel they *must* have—after all, everyone else has them!

3. The advertising industry has become more scientific and sophisticated. It seduces potential buyers of all income levels visually, with mood-enhancing music, and even aromas!

4. Credit has become ridiculously easy to obtain.

5. Concepts like restraint, frugality, delayed gratification, and self-discipline, which made perfect sense to previous generations, hold little appeal to people born after the mid-1950s. They want the good life now—whether they can afford it or not.

"IMAGE IS EVERYTHING!"

Another factor that plays a major role in the debt issue is image. In the early 1990s an emerging tennis star named Andre Agassi made a television commercial for Canon cameras that featured the message "Image is everything!"

Agassi was young, handsome, flashy, and a great athlete who was getting a lot of publicity at the time. He came across as shallow in the commercial, and he's lived to regret appearing in it for two reasons. First, it didn't portray who Agassi was, even in those days. Second, the concept of image being crucially important has had the wrong kind of staying power. Agassi, who is known for his kindness, generosity, and tireless work with disadvantaged youths, says it was simply a youthful mistake in judgment.

You can do your own informal study of TV commercials and see for yourself that a high percentage are aimed at people who want to improve their image. The pervasive message is that it's not what's on the inside that matters; it's how you *appear* to others. One I just love to hate is for a car rental company. It features a dorky-looking guy getting ready to go to his ten-year high school reunion. He wants to show up in style and make his former classmates think he's made it in the world (maybe he knows Stan the Mercedes Man). So he rents a fancy car for that one evening. Of course, when he drives up to the building, two gorgeous babes from his class just happen to be standing out by the curb. They ooh and ah over the car, conclude that he's a hunk with money, and fawn all over him. "Image is everything!"

Sadly, this message holds tremendous appeal for many people of all ages, and they're willing to go deeply into debt in order to look good. In the San Francisco area, where I live, the BMW is the car of choice among many young people, but they far outdo the guy in the car rental commercial. He only paid to rent that fancy car for one night and undoubtedly got the cheaper weekend rate. The BMW crowd want a car for *every* occasion, so they strap themselves financially for three to five years by either taking out a huge loan or signing a lease that squeezes them every month. "Image is everything!"

In the latter years of my high school teaching career, I heard several kids say they were embarrassed to ride in their family cars because they were so "lame" and "uncool." Even sadder was the fact that many of the parents bought more hip (and expensive) cars just to appease their kids and impress other kids. "Image is everything!"

Solomon would look at these cars and say, "Do not set your heart on ill-gotten gains, they will be of no use to you" (Ecclesiastes 5:8 JER), and Jesus would say, "Watch out! Be on your guard against all kinds of greed; a man's life does not consist in the abundance of his possessions" (Luke 12:15 NIV).

> *Never spend your money before you have it.*
> —THOMAS JEFFERSON

> *You can't always get what you want.*
> —THE ROLLING STONES

LIVING WITH LESS AND LOVING IT MORE

> *Man is rich in proportion to the number of things he can do without.*
> —HENRY DAVID THOREAU

I'm not going to suggest that we all need to take a vow of poverty and live in total austerity in order to be happy or to live in keeping with the teachings of the Scriptures. They don't tell us to do that. But they do tell us to resist the enticements of the material world, to be wise, to resist the worship of money and possessions, and to show restraint in financial matters. The single greatest source of the problem is that we think we need more than we really do. We think we need many things to be happy because we're bombarded daily with images of happy people whose condition seems directly related to having all the right things. That's the number one aim of the advertising industry—to create that connection in our brains between things and happiness—and it's been doing it effectively for many years. As soon as we think we need something, we go buy it. But that kind of thinking is shallow. It never gets below the surface. The Scriptures tell us to go a little deeper in our thinking, to ask ourselves what our *real* needs are, and to think about what's most important in life. When we do this, we can live more simply; we realize that there are a lot of things we can do without, and we enjoy life and what we have at a much deeper level.

> *Most of the luxuries, and many of the so-called comforts of life, are not only not indispensable, but positive hindrances to the elevation of man-kind. . . . Money is not required to buy one necessity of the soul.*
>
> —HENRY DAVID THOREAU

> *No matter how rich you become, how famous or powerful, when you die the size of your funeral will still pretty much depend on the weather.*
>
> —MICHAEL PRITCHARD

COMMANDMENT 3

DON'T USE DESTRUCTIVE LANGUAGE

IT HURTS OTHERS AS WELL AS YOURSELF

Old Testament Proverbs

Thoughtless words can wound like a sword...

—PROVERBS 12:18 JER

The mouth of the fool works its owner's ruin.

—PROVERBS 18:6 JER

New Testament

Do not let any unwholesome talk come out of your mouths.

—EPHESIANS 4:29 NIV

Commandment 3

Don't use destructive language
It hurts others as well as yourself

He who guards his lips guards his life, but he who speaks rashly will come to ruin.

—Proverbs 13:3 NIV

Two Pulitzer Prize Winners on the Power of Words

There's nothing more powerful, yet more unrecognized, than the power of words. There's a simple reason: we tend to take words for granted. They've been part of our everyday lives since long before we could talk, and they're the most basic tools we have for connecting with the rest of the world. Yet, just as fish are unaware that they're surrounded by water, we often seem unaware of the ocean of words in which we live. More important, we frequently forget that our words can have great impact on both the lives of others and our own. Two well-known and highly respected modern-day figures have eloquently pointed this out.

Will Durant (1885–1981) was arguably the greatest and most prolific historian of all time. For more than fifty years he and his wife, Ariel, worked on one book (11 volumes), *The Story of Civilization*. He won both the Pulitzer Prize and the Presidential Medal of Freedom for his contributions to our knowledge of history, culture, and philosophy. Durant was asked many times throughout his career what he considered to be the greatest achievements in the history of the human race. Who was more qualified to answer such a question? In a marvelous little book called *The Greatest Minds and Ideas of All Time,* he listed ten, which he called "peaks of progress." Among them were the development of science, education, and agriculture. Think where we'd be without them. But the most important of all, according to Durant, was the development of language—the spoken word. He says that without it none of the others would have been possible. Words have determined the course of history simply because they enable us to communicate our ideas to one another.

> *Throughout human history, our greatest leaders and thinkers have used the power of words to transform our emotions, to enlist us in their causes, and to shape the course of destiny. Words can not only create emotions, they create actions. And from our actions flow the results of our lives.*
>
> —TONY ROBBINS

> *Words are what hold society together; without them we should not be human beings.*
>
> —STUART CHASE

Maya Angelou, also a winner of the Pulitzer Prize and countless other awards, is often recognized as one of the most influential figures in contemporary literature. She's a poet, teacher, historian, civil rights activist, and the author of several best-selling books. And no one seems to understand more clearly the importance and the power of words. In 1993 she was interviewed by *USA Weekend* magazine about her perspective on language and the impact it can have. She said that most people look upon words as "ephemeral," thinking that they last for only a short period of time. But she's convinced that words are "tangible things"; we just don't have a way to accurately measure them. And, once said, they never die.

> *I do believe that words . . . go into the body, as effect. So they cause us to be well and hopeful and high energy and wondrous and funny and cheerful. Or they can cause us to be depressed. They get into the body and cause us to be sullen and sour and depressed and, finally, sick.*
>
> —Maya Angelou

Two Biblical Writers on the Power of Words

> *The tongue has the power of life and death.*
>
> —Proverbs 18:21 NIV

Long before Will Durant and Maya Angelou came along, wise old Solomon was writing his Proverbs. He wrote that an essential part of wisdom is in understanding the impact of our words on both others and on ourselves. He considered this so important that he wrote about it in more than fifty different verses (a teacher who knew how to drive home his point!). Here are a few of them:

From the fruit of his lips a man is filled with good things as surely as the work of his hands rewards him. (12:14 NIV)

Reckless words pierce like a sword, but the tongue of the wise brings healing. (12:18 NIV)

The tongue of the wise makes knowledge welcome, the mouth of the fool spews folly. (15:2 JER)

A tongue that brings healing is a tree of life, but a deceitful tongue crushes the spirit. (15:4 NIV)

A fool gets into constant fights. His mouth is his undoing! His words endanger him. (18:6–7 TLB)

A word aptly spoken is like apples of gold in settings of silver. (25:11 NIV)

Solomon wasn't alone in his belief. Throughout the Old and New Testaments there are repeated warnings and suggestions about the importance of what we say. One of the most vivid descriptions ever written about the power of the tongue can be found in the third chapter of the letter of James in the New Testament. He says, "The human tongue is physically small, but what tremendous effects it can boast of!" (James 3:5 PHI). To illustrate his point, he uses some vivid analogies:

- **A ship:** He reminds us of the enormous size of a ship and the momentum it gains with a fair wind behind it, and then points out that a tiny rudder controls the entire operation.

- **A horse:** This animal is much bigger, stronger, and faster than a human. But man can completely control a horse by placing a tiny bit inside its mouth.

- **A spark of fire:** That's all it takes to set an entire forest ablaze, and he reminds us that "the tongue is as dangerous as any fire, with vast potentialities for evil" (James 3:6 PHI).

- **Other creatures:** He says all the birds, animals, reptiles, and creatures of the sea can be tamed by man, "but no one can tame the human tongue. It is an evil always liable to break out, and the poison it spreads is deadly" (James 3:6 PHI).

AN EXAMPLE OF SPREADING POISON

Please reread the last six words by James in the above paragraph. Did you ever think you could spread a deadly poison with your tongue? Just by talking? Not only *can* we do it, we do it every day. In fact, people have been doing it for thousands of years in homes, at work, in schools and universities, at social events, even in places of worship. The most amazing thing is that the people spewing the poison are often unaware of the toxic atmosphere they create.

Here's a case in point: Some years ago, the high school where I first taught was closed down due to declining enrollment, and I joined the faculty of another school in the district. It was a difficult adjustment after teaching for sixteen years at a school I truly loved. One thing that eased the transition was an invitation I received during my first few days on the job. I was asked to join some staff members for coffee and casual conversation each morning. For the new guy on the scene, it was just the welcome mat I needed.

Spearheading this informal coffee club were two women secretaries. The invitation to join the group came from them, and they wanted to know everything about me. One of the first things to come up was my faith—they'd heard that I was a Christian. They wanted to confirm what they'd heard and wanted me to know that they were Christians too. They also wanted me to know that they were members of a wonderful Protestant church and were both very active in it. I was worshiping in a different Protestant church at that time, and they wanted to know all about it. All this seemed pretty innocent in the beginning. But things changed quickly.

Within the next few days they asked me about my divorce, which was both surprising and disappointing. As politely as I could, I told them it had occurred twelve years earlier, was a painful memory, and I didn't really want to relive it. They moved on to another topic I preferred to avoid—a woman they both knew whom I had previously dated. I told them I'd rather talk about Cathy, to whom I'd been married for only five months. They weren't as interested in her as they were my ex-wife or my ex-girlfriend. All of this was mildly disturbing, and unfortunately just the tip of the iceberg.

With each coffee break came more gossip, and it got more mean-spirited and vicious as it went along. I was disappointed and shocked. Although I didn't ask about the private lives of faculty and staff members, I was informed about who was divorced, who was dating whom, who was having problems with their kids or finances, and on and on it went. They also thought I should know about what some of the people at their church were going through, including the senior pastor's rocky relationship with his daughter. The morning coffee group was Gossip Central and couldn't have been more toxic. I was truly astounded at both the volume and the meanness of it.

It also created a serious dilemma. I needed to remove myself from this poisonous environment. But how could I do it gracefully? After all, these people had reached out to me. Another concern was whether I had a responsibility to confront these self-proclaimed Christian women regarding their poisonous gossip. I didn't know the Scriptures all that well at the time, but I did know that gossip was a no-no, and I was pretty sure that I'd read something about confronting fellow Christians when their behavior was inconsistent with their professed faith.

I did my homework first. I found twenty-five references to gossip and slander in the Bible, thirteen in the Old Testament, and twelve in the New Testament. The message was pretty much the same, regardless of verse: *Don't do it!* I also found a passage in the New Testament that said we have a duty to gently, privately, and without any "feeling of superiority," confront fellow Christians regarding their wrongdoing and help them get "back on the right path" (Galatians 6:1 PHI). Easier said than done! I thought long and hard about (1) how to remove myself gracefully from this toxic atmosphere and (2) how to confront these women gently and constructively. Both would be a challenge.

I told them that I needed to get more work done during my prep period in the morning, which was true. In fact, I often wondered when the two of them got any work done. Since their offices were quite a distance from my classroom, I bought a coffee maker and set it up in there. I told them they would be seeing less of me, but I appreciated the way they had reached out to me at the beginning of the year, when everything was new. I also made an appointment to talk to one of the two women, who seemed more open than her friend.

I told her I needed to talk to her about a subject that was a bit uncomfortable and hoped she would understand that my heart was in the right place. As gently as I could, I explained my concerns about the gossip and what the Scriptures said about it. I'll never forget her answer. She said, "Oh, I know we're not supposed to do it, but it's too hard to stop. Nobody's perfect, you know, and everybody gossips. It's just so much fun. And besides, we never hurt anyone." Not the response I was expecting. I cringed, especially at the "we never hurt anyone" part. Is it possible to gossip without hurting anyone?

Unfortunately, that wasn't the final chapter. In only a matter of weeks the grapevine was abuzz with the news that I'd turned my back on people who had reached out to me. Word had it that my problem was a superiority complex: I thought I was too good to associate with secretaries. On top of that, I was "holier than thou" and felt free to go around condemning other people. It was somewhat amusing, but mostly it was sad.

*In fact they easily become worse than lazy, and degenerate
into gossips and busybodies with dangerous tongues.*

— 1 TIMOTHY 5:13 PHI

*Deep down, we know that gossip, whether it is true or
untrue, is destructive. It sets a fire ablaze that neither the
gossiper nor the one being gossiped about can control.*

— PHIL WARE

PREVENTING THE SPREAD OF POISON

The main point in the story above is that people do indeed use
their tongues to spray deadly poison into the atmosphere, just
as James had written. Even more distressing, they do so without the slightest awareness of the negative pall they're casting.
And gossip is only one of the many ways in which we can poison the atmosphere. We've all heard the expression "pick your
poison." Sadly, people do pick not just one but several of them,
on a daily basis. It becomes a habit, and, without even knowing it, they go from home to school or work, dispersing toxins
into the atmosphere. They poison others but seem to be im-
mune themselves, as the two women at my school were. They
drove other people out of the group also but were blissfully unaware of the toxic environment they had created. The silver
lining was that they gave me a great idea for eliminating the
toxins in my classroom.

I kept thinking about the deadly poison James told us we
could spread with our tongues and how I'd experienced it in

the first few days at my new school. A somewhat comical picture kept popping into my head: I would go into the coffee room, and these two women would whip out aerosol cans of poison and start spewing it all over the room. What a great visual aid a spray can of poison would be to use in my classroom! I obviously couldn't use real bug spray, so I repurposed an empty can of bathroom deodorant. I drew a skull and crossbones on a piece of paper, wrote "POISON" underneath it, and wrapped it around the can. I couldn't wait to use it.

At the beginning of every school year I put a lot of time and energy into creating a positive environment in each of my classes. I told my students that goal number one for the year was to create a "caring community" in my classroom. Think what life would be like if we paid more attention to the words we use and how we say them, and concentrated more on turning our homes, schools, job sites, and places of worship into caring communities.

I asked my students whether they would want to learn in a toxic or nourishing environment. Most understood, but a few were confused because they didn't know the meaning of either word. And that was okay. A big part of getting an education is building a better vocabulary. After I explained the terms, they all agreed with one of my favorite sayings: "Nothing grows unless it's in a nourishing environment." Having established that, I asked them a simple question. I held up the can and asked, "Then do you agree with me that it would be harmful if any of us sprayed poison into the atmosphere of our class?" Several of my students looked alarmed—kids tend to be more literal than adults. One of them asked, "Why would anyone spray poison into a classroom?" Smiling, I answered, "Unfortunately, both students and teachers have been spraying poison into classrooms since the earliest days of schools. Would you like to know how they do it?" They did, and we began to make a list together.

Later the adult students in a communication class I taught at the university added to it, and I eventually compiled a list of thirty different ways in which we can spray poison with our tongues. We agreed to do all we could to eliminate them. One of my high school students suggested that we give the list a nickname that really made a statement. It only took a few minutes to hit upon the perfect one.

THE DIRTY THIRTY

I'll be forever grateful to my students for making a significant contribution to the writing of my second book, which is called *Positive Words, Powerful Results.* I wrote it for two simple reasons: (1) to remind people of the powerful impact their words can have and (2) to urge them to choose words that affirm and celebrate life. While I originally wanted to keep the entire book positive, I found it necessary to include one chapter that reminded people how destructive and long-lasting our words can be. It's the third chapter in the book and is aptly titled, "Words Can Hurt and Offend." The Dirty Thirty are in that chapter, but I don't want you to have to rush out and buy the book in order to read them, so I've included them here:

1. Bragging
2. Swearing and other gross-out language
3. Gossip

4. Angry words

5. Lies

6. Mean-spirited and hurtful words

7. Judgmental words

8. Playing "poor me"—the self-pity game

9. Making discouraging remarks

10. Embarrassing and humiliating others

11. Excessive fault-finding and criticism

12. Complaining, whining, moaning, groaning

13. Rude and inconsiderate language

14. Teasing

15. Using words to manipulate others

16. Phony and insincere compliments, flattery

17. Ethnic and racial slurs

18. Sexist comments

19. Age-related put-downs

20. Being negative—always pointing out what's wrong

21. Threats

22. Arguing

23. Interrupting—not letting the other person finish

24. Playing "trump"—always topping someone else's story

25. Being a know-it-all

26. Sarcasm

27. Yelling, screaming

28. Talking down to people—being condescending

29. Exaggerating, blowing things out of proportion

30. Blaming and accusing others

We had quite a discussion after completing our list, which was longer than any of us had expected. One of my adults at the university seemed to sum it up best when she said, "I guess I never realized there were so many ways to spray poison into our environment. We really do need to pay more attention to what comes out of our mouths." The list helps us understand more clearly why Solomon advised us to guard our lips and James warned us of the poison we could spread with our tongues.

I asked both groups of students what implications the list had for their lives outside the classroom. My high school students said it made them more aware of how careless we are with our words and how easy it is to get into negative verbal ruts. They also suggested that students should be taught at an early age about the impact of words and that the lesson should be reinforced throughout their years in school. One of my students suggested that we sign a pledge not to spray poison into the atmosphere of the classroom. I thought it was a great idea, as did the other students, and by the next day we had all signed the "No Poison Pledge." Putting our commitment down on paper was remarkably effective.

My adult students had a slightly different perspective. They all worked full-time, many in management positions in high-tech Silicon Valley industries. Most of them wanted to concentrate on removing the poison in their workplaces. Having spent my entire professional career in classrooms, I was amazed to learn how much poison hangs in the offices and meeting rooms of corporate America—especially complaining, criticism, blaming, and gossip. One student suggested we make a Dirty Thirty poster to be prominently displayed in every workplace building. Everyone in the class agreed that it would be a good idea. They were also in agreement that the list has implications for home as well. They concurred that most people "let it all hang out" when they get home, effectively spreading poison from the workplace to the place where they live.

The Heart and the Tongue

Good people draw what is good from the store of goodness in their hearts; bad people draw what is bad from the store of badness. For the words of the mouth flow out of what fills the heart.

—LUKE 6:45 JER

The word "heart" has several meanings. *Merriam-Webster's Collegiate Dictionary* includes these among them: "one's innermost character, feelings, or inclinations; the central or innermost part; the essential or most vital part of something." So we're not talking about the organ that pumps blood through our vascular system. As it's used in this context, the heart is the core of every human being. Therefore, if what comes out of our mouths is from what's stored in our hearts, our words are incredibly revealing. What *is* coming out of our mouths? If there's too much negativity coming out, we need to look inside and ask ourselves why we have so much negativity stored up. How did it get there?

Well, we put it there, and then we harbored it. Keep in mind the title of the first chapter of this book: "Don't be seduced by popular culture." One of the things popular culture, particularly some elements of the media, does is fill our minds and hearts with garbage—angry, filthy, disrespectful, negative ideas. That sounds as though I'm condemning all media, and I don't mean to do that. It does offer plenty of ways to nurture ourselves also. But if we choose to put the junk it offers into our heads and hearts, it will eventually come out of our mouths. This is the origin of the so-called Freudian slip. Freud said that what's stored in our minds (hearts) will eventually slip off the tongue. He believed he had made a great discovery when he presented this theory, but long before he came along, King David, Solomon, Jesus, James, and several other biblical figures had already told us the same thing.

Zig Ziglar, the well-known motivational speaker from Texas, has a knack for catchy phrases. They're full of common sense, and they quickly capture our attention. One I shared year after year with my students is "You are what you are because of what goes into your mind." While many don't immediately grasp its meaning, they come to understand it perfectly after a brief discussion. The mind is the control center—garbage in, garbage out. If we allow the media and other people to put negative things into our minds, our words will eventually reveal what we've stored inside. From the overflow of the heart the mouth speaks.

In his wonderful book *Words That Hurt, Words That Heal,* Rabbi Joseph Telushkin explains how he challenges people to go twenty-four hours without saying anything negative about another person. He says if you can't do it, "then you've lost control over your tongue." Sadly, too many people *have* lost control of their tongues. We live in a culture of complaints, put-downs, gossip, criticism, blaming, foul language, and other items straight off the Dirty Thirty. They enter our minds and hearts from a variety of sources, and they eventually roll off of our tongues.

I've been issuing a challenge similar to Rabbi Telushkin's for many years. Starting in 1972, I began asking my high school students if they could go one full day without complaining. Their response? They complained that it was too hard. A few called it impossible and didn't even want to try. I convinced them that it was worth the effort even if they couldn't go a full twenty-four hours because they would learn something about themselves. They did try and failed miserably: Many of them couldn't go five minutes without complaining. But as I predicted, they *did* learn something about themselves. They had no idea how often they complained and now realized that it had become a habit with a powerful hold on them.

I also issued the same challenge to my adult students at the university, thinking they would have an easier time of it. Wrong. They couldn't do it either. But I didn't give up and continued to challenge both groups of students every year from then on. It took twenty-three years to find someone who could do it. The winner was a high school junior named Grace. She said she was able to do it with the help of a technique she had devised herself. Every time she started to complain, which was often, she instead wrote down something or someone she was thankful for. She showed me her list. It had more than twenty-five things on it. She articulated something I've believed for many years: "Even though we live in a culture in which we have so much more to be thankful for than we have to complain about, we complain a hundred times more than we express thanks." And we poison the atmosphere every time we do.

One of the simple principles of life that we need to remind ourselves of on a daily basis is this: every time we open our mouths, we reveal something about ourselves. Our words reveal what's stored in our hearts. They reveal our character, who we really are. If our words are frequently negative and angry, we'll not only pollute the atmosphere but drive people away from us. We reap what we sow.

> *Speech is the mirror of the soul; as a man speaks, so he is.*
> —PUBLIUS SYRUS

TWO IMPORTANT CHOICES REGARDING OUR WORDS

One of the central themes of all my writing is a single word: *Choices.* I raised it in my first book in a chapter entitled "We Live by Choice, Not by Chance." My second book included a chapter called "Words Are Choices." And it was reinforced in the title of my third book, *Choices That Change Lives.* Sometimes it's more important to be reminded than it is to be informed, and most of us need daily reminders that everything we do is a choice. This is especially important when applied to our words. We make two important choices:

1. Whether to speak or remain silent

> *The real art of conversation is not only to say the right thing in the right place, but far more difficult still, to leave unsaid the wrong thing at the tempting moment.*
> —DOROTHY NEVILL

He who holds his tongue is wise.

—PROVERBS 10:19 NIV

"Put your mind in gear before you put your mouth in motion"—it's easy to remember and understand but a lot more difficult to practice. Most of us are guilty of saying stupid or offensive things on more occasions than we'd like to recall simply because we didn't take a few seconds to think first. A mentor of mine once told me, "If I had a dollar for every time I spoke foolishly without thinking first, I'd probably be on the Forbes Richest People list." That actually made me feel pretty good because he was one of the wisest people I'd ever known, and until then I'd thought I was the only one who felt like that. It's astounding how many problems we can cause for ourselves and others when we speak rashly, when we don't put our minds in gear first. This particular mentor, like many others, said he had had to learn the hard way. In other words, from his mistakes. A true sign of wisdom, he said, is knowing when to listen, when to speak, and when to hold your tongue—exactly what Solomon said back in the tenth century B.C.

2. Whether to use nourishing or toxic words

The mouth of the righteous is a fountain of life, but
violence overwhelms the mouth of the wicked.

—PROVERBS 10:11 NIV

Whatever words we utter should be chosen with care, for
people will hear them and be influenced by them for good or ill.

—BUDDHA

I grew up in a polluted atmosphere. I don't mean near a factory that pumped chemical toxins into the air or near a plant that discharged contaminants into the water supply. I mean my home. Although my mother is the sweetest person you could ever meet and always has something kind and affirming to say, it was my father who made all the noise in the family. And sadly, he was the angriest and most negative person I've ever known. Although honest, hardworking, law-abiding, and generous with his time and resources, he had little control over his tongue. He was confrontational, loud, and critical. In addition, he both complained and swore a lot, usually at the same time. At the top of his list were politicians, especially Richard Nixon (whom he was still complaining about twenty years after Nixon's death), and his favorite phrase was the name of God with the words "damn it" tacked onto it. Unfortunately, I grew up thinking "this is how men talk," and my own language was negatively influenced by it. Apparently, I got more of my father's genes than I did my mother's.

Fortunately, my college education had a profound effect on my speech patterns in two ways. First, I found myself surrounded by intelligent, educated men (all my undergraduate professors were male) who spoke gently and positively, and it dawned on me at age seventeen that my father was the exception, not the rule. Second, the Jesuits at the University of San Francisco were big on teaching and reminding us that we had been given a free will, the power of choice. And that included the power to choose the words we used and the way we said them.

It took some time, but both my vocabulary and my manner of speaking improved dramatically. Early in my teaching career I had another illuminating experience regarding the impact of words. I became close friends with a colleague who changed my life dramatically. His name is Tim Hansel, and I've mentioned him in previous books. In a nutshell, Tim *always* had something good to say. Everything that came out of his mouth was positive. He looked for the good, found the good, and talked about the good. You won't be surprised to hear that he was a joy to be around.

I asked Tim early in our friendship how he had gotten that way. His upbringing had been markedly different from mine. Both his mother and father had been positive, upbeat, and funny people, and he had those qualities in spades. I'm convinced they were part of his nature and nurtured by his home environment. As a child he also learned some valuable lessons from the Scriptures. One of them was about the power of words. He quoted David, Solomon, Jesus, Paul, and James. At that time I had limited knowledge of these men and their teachings, so Tim bought me my first Bible. I was a nonbeliever at that time, but I read it because it was a gift from a special friend. I was amazed at the good advice and common sense that it contained. And I was surprised at how often it referred to the power of the tongue.

Tim was an in-the-flesh example of the happy result of choosing the right words. We feel better, and we make other people feel better. We spread joy instead of poison. Everyone loved Tim and wanted to be around him. He was a walking testament to the axiom that we reap what we sow.

Do not let any unwholesome talk come out of your mouths, but only what is helpful for building others up according to their needs, that it may benefit those who listen.

—EPHESIANS 4:29 NIV

Pleasant words are a honeycomb, sweet to the soul and healing to the bones.

—PROVERBS 16:24 NIV

COMMANDMENT 4

DON'T JUDGE OTHER PEOPLE

IT'S BETTER TO WORK ON YOUR OWN FAULTS

Old Testament Proverb

Who can say, "I have kept my heart pure; I am clean and without sin"?

—PROVERBS 20:9 NIV

New Testament

Why do you look at the speck of sawdust in your brother's eye and pay no attention to the plank in your own eye?

—MATTHEW 7:3 NIV

COMMANDMENT 4

DON'T JUDGE OTHER PEOPLE
IT'S BETTER TO WORK ON YOUR OWN FAULTS

*Now if you feel inclined to set yourself up as a judge of
those who sin, let me assure you, whoever you are, that you
are in no position to do so. For at whatever point you
condemn others you automatically condemn yourself, since
you, the judge, commit the same sins.*

—ROMANS 2:1 PHI

ONE OF THE BIBLE'S MOST CHALLENGING COMMANDS

As mentioned in the introduction, some of the things the Scriptures advise us to do (or not do) are enormous challenges. Some
of them might even seem impossible. But they're not. It all depends on how hard we're willing to work at correcting our flaws.
While someone else may have a different opinion, I think obey-
ing the command not to judge others is the second toughest
challenge contained in the Bible. What is number one? You'll
find it in a succeeding chapter. But don't skip ahead. The challenge in this chapter is more than enough for now.

Why is it so difficult to refrain from judging others? There are two reasons. First, we're all born with the basic flaw mentioned in the introduction to this section: *pride*. There's no nice way of saying it—we're simply all conceited, self-centered, egotistical, vain, and selfish. As harsh as this may sound, it's a reality we struggle with all our lives. We come into the world flawed—it's the human condition. But the good news is that we also have free will, the ability to choose. Ultimately, our success in life will be determined by how we choose to handle our pride, to what degree we conquer it. The people who manage to do this spend very little of their time and energy judging others.

The second reason it's so hard to not judge others is that it easily becomes a habit. It becomes a habit because we live in a culture in which we're surrounded by complaining, criticizing, blaming, judging, and even condemning. We're affected by it at work, in social circles, at home, and, saddest of all, in places of worship. To top it all off, the media bombard us with their judgments daily. We get sucked in without even realizing it's happening to us. Judging others has almost become a sport, and there are even those (celebrity gossip blogs, anyone?) who strive to be better at it than anyone else. To some people, there's nothing more fun than talking about someone else's faults. It's so commonplace that it's become acceptable.

WHY DO WE JUDGE OTHERS?

*Most of our censure of others is only oblique praise of self,
uttered to show the wisdom and superiority of the speaker.*
—TYRON EDWARDS

During my many years as a teacher I was faced with a challenge each September as the school year began: how to deal effectively with the apparently irresistible pull teenagers feel to put one another down. As explained in the previous chapter, when invited, my students helped me keep out most of the poison from the classroom, but it took quite a few years before I came up with the idea. It was much more difficult early in my career, but I felt a strong need to come up with a solution for the simple reason that the put-downs were detrimental to anyone's learning anything. Nothing grows in a toxic environment.

The first time I confronted the problem, I was teaching a group of ninth-graders. I simply asked them why they criticized one another so often. Their answers were both amusing and enlightening. One piped up with "Because this school has so many lame people in it." Another quickly followed with "Some of the kids who go here can be so annoying." And a third: "People at this school are in major need of a clue. They're just so un-cool." Then came the best comment of all from Ian, an incredibly bright, perceptive, and funny fourteen-year-old: "Isn't it a shame that everyone can't be as cool as we are?" Some of the kids got it, some didn't. His comment was the springboard for a great discussion about why we criticize, judge, and put down one another. By the time we were finished everyone was in on the joke.

Part of the discussion was about psychology, which I was teaching to twelfth-graders at the time. Many of these ninth-graders weren't even sure what it was. To keep things simple, I defined psychology as the study of human behavior and explained that its purpose is to help us understand why people do what they do. As in, why do we put each other down so much? I asked them if they had ever heard of Sigmund Freud. A few had, most hadn't. I told them he is often considered to be the father of psychology. Then I asked if they had ever heard of Carl Jung, another pioneer in the field. No one had. So I wrote the following on the chalkboard:

> *Everything that irritates us about others can lead us to an understanding of ourselves.*
>
> —CARL JUNG

I asked them what they thought he meant. One of the kids said it sounded like something his mother had told him. She'd said, "What we don't like about other people is usually what we don't like about ourselves." Another student offered this: "Every time you point your finger at someone else, you're pointing three back at yourself." It seems that this wisdom has been passed down for generations, but it still doesn't stop us from judging others. Like the Golden Rule, we understand perfectly what it means, but it's a little more difficult to put it into practice.

Later that same day that I had this discussion with my ninth-grade students, I had a similar one with a group of professionals who were mostly in their thirties and forties. They were my students in a course at the university called Communication and Interpersonal Relations. When I asked them why we judge, criticize, and put down other people, their responses echoed the kids'. They didn't use the words "lame, clueless, and un-cool," but they did agree that many people are "annoying." In essence, there wasn't much difference between those at or approaching midlife and my younger charges. They knew who Freud and Jung were, all right, and they'd heard all the familiar phrases about what we're really doing when we judge others and agreed with them. Rich, a fifty-year-old police supervisor, said, "We know all the reasons why we're not supposed to judge others, but we do it anyway. It's good to be reminded how that works against you in a class like this. It would make us better managers if we'd apply what we've been taught."

We evaluate others with a Godlike justice, but we want them to evaluate us with a Godlike compassion.

—Sydney J. Harris

In judging others a man labors in vain; he often errs. . . . But in judging and examining himself he always labors to good purpose.

—Thomas à Kempis

For if you refuse to act kindly, you can hardly expect to be treated kindly. Kind mercy wins over harsh judgment every time.

—James 2:13 MES

Let us therefore stop turning critical eyes on one another. If we must be critical, let us be critical of our own conduct.

—Romans 14:13 PHI

A LITTLE TEST

Imagine you're just meeting someone who fits each of the descriptions below—what are your initial thoughts?

- Has ten to twenty tattoos—one in bright colors that covers an entire arm.

- Weighs between 300 and 400 pounds.

- Has several facial piercings, including nose, lip, and eyebrow.

- Wears black dress shoes and long black socks with shorts.

- Is in tattered clothing and pushing a shopping cart of belongings.

- Is physically unattractive.

Let's say you've just met someone who does one of the following—what would you think about that person?

- Makes several grammatical errors while talking.

- Talks loudly on a cell phone in a restaurant.

- Makes a stupid mistake in front of you while driving.

- Expresses strong political beliefs in direct opposition to yours.

- Plays video games more than six hours a day.

- Gets sloppy drunk.

If you're completely honest, you'll admit that you've passed judgment on at least a few people who fit the descriptions above. The list was pretty easy to compile. All I had to do was ask myself a simple question: On what occasions have I judged people without knowing all the facts? At various times in my life, I've been guilty of judging people in all of the above circumstances. It didn't bother me to do this when I was younger. But as I grew wiser and became more aware of my pride, I realized that every time I judged other people I was elevating myself above them—and I felt ugly inside. These are often called snap judgments, the kind the Scriptures tell us not to make. Nothing good can come from them.

I'm not saying you have to like or accept everything another person does. But because a person looks unappealing held against your standards or does something that annoys you, it doesn't mean he or she is a blight on humanity. I'll admit that I have trouble with people who use cell yell (that is, talk loudly on cell phones) in public places, especially in restaurants. I still think it's rude, but I can't conclude that the person is a total jerk. He or she could be a very loving and giving person who slips from time to time, just like millions of other people—or whose phone reception is just remarkably bad.

H. A. Ironside (1876–1951) was a well-known Bible teacher and the author of some sixty books. His *Illustrations of*

Bible Truth tells a story about a man called Bishop Potter and the folly of judging others:

> He was sailing for Europe on one of the great transatlantic ocean liners. When he went on board, he found out that another passenger was to share the cabin with him. After going to see the accommodations, he came to the purser's desk and inquired if he could leave his gold watch and other valuables in the ship's safe. He explained that ordinarily he never availed himself of that privilege, but he had been to his cabin and met the man who was to occupy the other berth. Judging from his appearance, he was afraid that he might not be a very trustworthy person. The purser accepted the responsibility for the valuables and remarked, "It's all right, Bishop, I'll be very glad to take care of them for you. The other man has been up here and left his for the same reason."

For a reason we may never understand, it seems much easier to jump to false and negative conclusions about another person than it is to assume that he or she is good, kind, and honest. Too often we make snap judgments and ascribe bad qualities to someone when we have only limited information. Once again, we're revealing something about ourselves. The faults we see in others are often a reflection of the faults we see when we look in the mirror. And if we see only faults, we can't see the good.

> *Judgment prevents us from seeing the good that lies beyond appearances.*
> —WAYNE DYER

IS ALL JUDGMENT WRONG?

In both the Old and New Testaments we're told to not judge others. There are many different kinds of judgment, but the Scriptures warn against only one of them. In *Merriam-Webster's Collegiate Dictionary* there are six definitions of the word "judge" as a verb. The first one is "to form an opinion about through careful weighing of evidence and testing of premises." This is not the type of judging the Bible warns us against. Another definition of "judge" in the same dictionary is "to form a negative opinion about." A synonym given for this type of judging is "guess." An example is also provided. We're told that we "shouldn't judge him because of his accent." The writers of the dictionary could have chosen several other examples, because people are judged daily based on everything from religion to race, age to sexual preference, political beliefs to education, occupation, and appearance, to mention just a few. This is a completely different kind of judgment. When we judge in this manner, we have only a small amount of information, and we use it to put another person down while elevating ourselves. This is what the Scriptures tell us is wrong.

There's a story in the Gospel of Luke that makes this point perfectly:

> *Two men went up to the temple to pray, one a Pharisee and the other a tax collector. The Pharisee stood up and prayed about himself, "God, I thank you that I am not like other men—robbers, evildoers, adulterers—or even like this tax collector. I fast twice a week and give a tenth of all I get."*

But the tax collector stood at a distance. He would not even look up to heaven, but beat his breast and said, "God, have mercy on me, a sinner." I tell you that this man, rather than the other, went home justified before God. For everyone who exalts himself will be humbled, and he who humbles himself will be exalted.

—LUKE 18:9–14 NIV

The Scriptures don't tell us that *all* judgment is wrong. In fact, our society couldn't survive *without* some forms of judgment. There are circumstances in which judgment is absolutely necessary. Here are a few examples:

- Our criminal justice system relies heavily on a person we call a judge. He or she is often assisted by citizens serving on a jury. Together, they study the evidence, share their perspectives, and reach a verdict.

- Teachers throughout the country, whether in elementary schools or medical schools, are required to evaluate the work of their students.

- In every business and profession people are hired, promoted, and fired on a regular basis. Someone has to make these critical judgments in order to ensure a successful operation.

- Consumers pass judgment on products and services every day. This is a crucial aspect of our free enterprise system. They vote with their dollars and by recommending (or not) products and services to others.

- Our democratic system of government also relies on the judgment of voters. We go to the polls frequently to make decisions about who is the best candidate for office or what is right or wrong about a ballot issue.

- All forms of competition require judgment. Someone has to pick Academy Award winners, members of the All-Star Team, and the most valuable player in the league.

- Publishers and editors judge the work of authors every day. They decide whether or not to publish the work of thousands of hopeful writers every year.

It isn't the act of judging that's wrong but the attitude with which it's done. Each time we look down upon someone else for a superficial reason, we're in essence saying the same thing my fourteen-year-old students were saying: "You're not cool because you're not like me." We have no right to judge other people in this way. That's why Solomon asks us if we are clean and without sin and Jesus asks us why we see the speck in our neighbor's eye so clearly but fail to see the plank in our own. When we judge others in this way, we dishonor the Scriptures, ignore principles of common sense, and in the end reap just what we have sown.

> *Do not judge, or you too will be judged. For in the same*
> *way you judge others, you will be judged, and with the*
> *measure you use, it will be measured to you.*
> —MATTHEW 7:1 NIV

"I'm Saved, and You're Not"

The whole problem with the world is that fools and fanatics are always so certain of themselves, and wiser people so full of doubts.

—Bertrand Russell

All of us have a "hot button" or two. The term is so common that it's now in the dictionary. Here's the way *Merriam-Webster* defines it: "an emotional and usually controversial issue or concern that triggers immediate intense reaction." Many of the common hot buttons in this country involve politics. Sometimes particular politicians can be hot buttons, as Richard Nixon was for my father. In more recent years Bill Clinton has been known to raise the heart rates of conservative Republicans the same way George W. Bush makes many a liberal Democrat's blood boil. Other hot buttons include specific political issues such as abortion, gay marriage, the death penalty, our tax laws, and prayer in school.

It could be a particular type of rude behavior, such as talking loudly on a cell phone in a public place. Sometimes a celebrity with strong views becomes a hot button for many people. The name Jane Fonda comes immediately to mind. Even well-known religious figures can become hot buttons. For many fundamentalist Christians it's the pope, no matter who holds the position. For others it could be Pat Robertson, Jerry Falwell, or both. Even a baseball team can become a hot button—just ask Red Sox or Yankee fans. Or, if you're on the West

Coast, ask Giants or Dodgers fans. Lots of different things can get us fired up.

I have a few hot buttons, just as we all do. Some cell phone behavior ranks pretty high on my list, but it pales in comparison to what holds the number one spot. I debated whether or not I should share this in writing, but several of my readers have written to tell me how much they appreciate my honesty and transparency. A hospital supervisor in Iowa wrote, "It's nice to know that authors who write these kinds of book are willing to admit their own weaknesses and struggles." A graduate student in New York wrote, "It really helps your readers to know you have flaws, too. Thanks for not always playing it safe." I treasure comments like these. They help me know that I'm connecting with my reading audience. So I want to be transparent, real, and honest on this issue also.

My number one hot button is overzealous and ultrarighteous Christian fundamentalists who judge and condemn people of other faiths and different viewpoints. Whether it's implicitly or explicitly stated, the message that gets me is this one: "Only my literal and narrow interpretation of what's written in the Scriptures is correct. Unless you believe exactly as I do, you can't be saved. I'm saved, and you're not." These people have no shortage of targets: Catholics, Mormons, Jews, and even some Protestant denominations. Beyond religious groups, their primary targets are agnostics, homosexuals, Planned Parenthood, the ACLU, and liberals in general. The amount of anger, hatred, judgment, and condemnation they demonstrate is truly frightening. In my opinion, they do far more harm to the cause of Christianity than they do good. It's hard to find the love of God in either their message or their manner. I've always been under the impression that they've missed some important passages in the Bible. Like this one:

> *We shall all be judged one day, not by each other's standards or even by our own, but by the judgment of God.*
> —ROMANS 14:1 PHI

A dear friend of mine who's not a believer made this comment to me a few years ago: "I don't understand how you can be a Christian. They're so damn close-minded and self-righteous. They condemn everyone who doesn't see things exactly as they do. If that's Christianity, I don't want to have anything to do with it. How can you be part of all that?" I answered, "I'm not part of all that. You're stereotyping—you're lumping us all together, when the truth is that there's a wide variety of people who profess to be Christians. I don't like the type you're talking about any more than you do. In fact, they embarrass me. They repel people rather than draw them to God as they're called to do."

He admitted that he was guilty of stereotyping, but he had another point he wanted to make. "How about all this 'saved' stuff? I get pretty sick of hearing them assign so many people to Hell. You can't tell me that a loving person like Gandhi is burning in Hell, and that the Dalai Lama is headed there too." I said, "No, I can't tell you that. It's not something I even think about. It's not my responsibility as a Christian to decide who goes to Heaven and who doesn't. In fact, the Scriptures specifically forbid me to do it. That decision is God's, and *only* God's."

I had a similar discussion over the phone with another dear

friend while I was in the midst of writing this chapter. He called me about the work we do together in character education. Before we got into that, though, he asked what I'd been up to, and I told him I was working on another book. "What's this one about?" he asked. I said it was about the challenge of applying the Scriptures to everyday life. That lit a fire in him somewhere. "I'd still be Christian if more of them would practice what they preach." This is a bright, loving, ethical man who claims to have been "driven away by the close-minded, judgmental fanatics." He added, "That's why our country is so divided right now." Then he said something that I'd never heard before but understood completely. He said, "I love Christ and his teachings, but I *hate* Christianity." It reminded me of something Gandhi once said: "I like your Christ, I do not like your Christians. Your Christians are so unlike your Christ."

The Christian ideal has not been tried and found wanting;
it has been found difficult and left untried.
—G. K. Chesterton

When Christians
Judge and Bash One Another

You were all called to travel on the same road and in the same
direction, so stay together, both outwardly and inwardly. You have
one Master, one faith, one baptism, one God and Father of all, who
rules over all, works through all, and is present in all.
—Ephesians 4:4–6 MES

I grew up thinking that all Christians, regardless of denomination, were respectful and tolerant of one another because they worshiped the same God. I was naïve. Somehow, I was shielded for many years from Christians bashing one another, so I was both shocked and saddened when I encountered it for the first time. And it saddened me even more to learn that it goes on regularly.

I was raised a Catholic and remained one until I was twenty-nine years old. In all those years of attending Catholic schools and going to Mass on Sunday, I never once heard a priest or a nun say anything derogatory about other faiths, Christian or non-Christian. To do that would have seemed inconsistent with the message of Christianity. The only remark I ever heard in connection with Protestants was a respectful reference to them as "our separated brothers and sisters." There was no judgment passed on them, no declaration about whether they were "saved" or not.

After a ten-year hiatus from both God and religion, I resurfaced in a Presbyterian church. I was a member for eighteen years and never once heard a pastor say anything negative about another faith. Again, I thought that was the way things were supposed to be. During the period that I served as an elder in that church I read some things in the newspaper that I found appalling. Pat Robertson, the well-known TV evangelist, said that Episcopalians, Methodists, and Presbyterians were associated with "the spirit of the Antichrist." At around the same time Jerry Falwell, another TV evangelist, said, "If you're not a born-again Christian, you're a failure as a human being." He also said that Christians should be running our government and all our schools.

I hadn't been a Protestant very long, and I found these pro-
nouncements both disappointing and befuddling. Why would
high-profile Christian figures make such outrageous, inflam-
matory comments? They seemed inconsistent with what the
Scriptures say about judging others. I needed a little help in
understanding all of this, so I made an appointment with the
senior pastor. He said he found their comments disappointing
too, because they didn't reflect Christianity as he'd learned it.
He said, "There's a wide spectrum of beliefs within the Christian community, just as there's a wide range of political beliefs
within a given party; we don't always agree on everything."

I told him I was glad that he didn't bash other churches. He
said, "We don't do that because the Bible tells us not to. Besides that, nothing good can ever come from it. Our mission is
to save souls, not pass judgment on what other people believe."
He said that on the day he had become senior pastor, he had
insisted on two firm "nevers": (1) Never criticize another faith
or denomination and (2) never tell parishioners how to vote on
either a political candidate or a political issue. He said, "All it
does is stir up trouble. We think people should be left to think
for themselves."

I wish leaders in all faiths embraced the same policy, but unfortunately they don't, and I've heard some disturbing things in
recent years. The first was from a pastor friend who constantly
bashed the Mormons. This otherwise even-keeled man got visibly
agitated whenever the subject came up. He would raise his voice
and say, "They're a cult!" adding, "A *dangerous* cult!" This was before he launched into a scathing criticism of their core beliefs. I
found this disturbing because I have several Mormon friends, and
I respect both them and what they believe. Some of our beliefs are

different, but we also share many, such as those about how we should conduct our lives. I also found my pastor friend's attack on Mormons illogical. What difference does it make what people of another faith believe if they're not harming us in any way?

His comments about Mormons were at least made in private. What's far more upsetting is when pastors bash other denominations from the pulpit. I've experienced it in two different churches, and have heard similar stories from a number of friends. In all these cases, the target was the Catholic Church. One pastor got more fired up about Catholics than my friend did about Mormons, and he shared his thoughts with an entire congregation. Among other things, he said that Catholics couldn't be saved because their entire religion was based on "false doctrine." Another time he simply made fun of the Catholic Church while again using the word "saved," and a third time he said Catholics weren't Christians because they worship Mary. Despite some Protestant churches' long-held beliefs, Catholics do *not* worship Mary.

Try to imagine being a Catholic who happened to attend that service as the leader of the church taught his followers things that were patently false, bashed the Catholic faith, and condemned its followers to Hell. Ironically, a line in the mission statement of his church claims that it is a "fellowship of believers among whom God is breaking down walls that have divided Christians for far too long." God may be breaking down walls, but the pastor seemed intent on building bigger ones. Another passage says: "We are a nondenominational church that encourages fellowship and unity among all believers regardless of denominational affiliation." Attacking the Catholic Church is a form of "fellowship and unity"?

In the other Protestant church I've attended, the pastor is a former Catholic. Having left the church for a few decades myself, I have no problem with this. I feel people should worship in a place in which they're comfortable and in which they can grow in their faith. The ex-Catholic pastor in this case is a humble, gentle, and sincere Christian. He's also young and somewhat new at being a lead pastor. Just as I made mistakes in my early years of teaching, he's made a few mistakes as he was starting out.

He told his congregation that Catholics worship Mary (still wrong), that they believe they can work their way into Heaven (also wrong), and that he wasn't "saved" when he was a Catholic. Imagine again how uncomfortable any Catholic would be hearing those words. I wrote him a letter expressing my concerns, and, to his credit, he was open to criticism and sincere in his desire to grow both as a Christian and as a pastor. He graciously asked to meet with me.

The main point I tried to make with him was that nothing good can come from Christians criticizing people of other denominations or faiths. I explained the no-bashing policy of my previous Protestant pastor and suggested that he consider adopting a similar one. He assured me that he would.

I wasn't looking for any type of victory in meeting with him. I simply wanted to help him understand that what he was saying in church was inconsistent with biblical teachings about judging others. I admired him for his openness and his willingness to listen to me. I also appreciated his apology, even though I wasn't looking for one. We agreed that day that our core beliefs were the same, though we may differ on some minor points of doctrine, and I walked away from our meeting with feelings of deep respect for both him and his faith. I hope he felt the same. How I wish people of different faiths would talk more often about their common beliefs and the ways in which they could work together.

> *It is not for us to say who, in the deepest sense, is or is not close to the spirit of Christ. We do not see into men's hearts. We cannot judge, and are indeed forbidden to judge. It would be wicked arrogance for us to say that any man is, or is not, a Christian in this refined sense.*
>
> —C. S. LEWIS

When I hear people of one faith pass judgment on what people of other faiths believe, the same questions always pop up: Does this serve any useful purpose? Does it bring people closer to God? Does it build unity within the community of believers? Does it help people align their lives better to the teachings of the Scriptures? The answers never change, no matter how many times these questions arise. The answer to all of them is a resounding *No.* A few other questions also come to mind: Is it wrong to criticize others for what they believe? Does it violate the teachings of the Scriptures? Does it give Christianity a bad name? Does it drive some people away from the faith? And no matter how many times these questions come up, the answer to all of them is *Yes.*

> *Make it your aim to be at one in the Spirit, and you will inevitably be at peace with one another.*
>
> —EPHESIANS 4:3 PHI

It is in America's best interests to understand one another and to find as much common ground as possible.

—JIMMY CARTER

LEARNING NOT TO JUDGE

In the Jewish tradition the holiest day of the year is Yom Kippur, the Day of Atonement. It's also called Yom Hadin, the Day of Judgment. This great holy day is a time for people to put everything else aside and devote themselves to serious reflection and introspection. They consider their sins of the past year and whom they've sinned against. Part of the day is spent thinking about how they may have judged others wrongly. In many ways it's a day of cleansing—freeing oneself from one's sins, learning from them, and growing beyond them.

Several years ago I heard a sermon about repentance and forgiveness. The pastor suggested that the atoning Jews' practice on Yom Kippur should be practiced by people of all faiths on a daily basis. He suggested a "time of atonement" at the end of each day in which we ask ourselves some simple questions: In what ways did I dishonor the Scriptures today? Whom did I sin against? Whom did I wrongly judge? How can I do better tomorrow? A simple technique like this, if practiced regularly, is remarkably effective in limiting how often we judge others wrongly.

Another great lesson we can learn from Jewish teachings is to look upon all people from a different perspective. Rabbis teach that we should judge every person *l'kaf zehut,* which means letting the positive outweigh the negative. In the rabbinic tradition, judging people in this manner is an important aspect of wisdom. Instead of focusing on outward appearance, this practice encourages us to look at the heart. And then we learn from others instead of judging them.

> *Who is the person who is wise? The one who has the ability to learn something from every person. A wise person is able to really hear and appreciate that every individual can make a valuable contribution to our life, to our community.*
> —RABBI JEFFREY SUMMIT

> *The Lord does not look at the things man looks at. Man looks at outward appearance, but the Lord looks at the heart.*
> —1 SAMUEL 16:7 NIV

> *Remember that I'm Human. Before you judge me or decide how you'll deal with me, walk awhile in my shoes. If you do, I think you'll find with more understanding we can meet in the middle and walk the rest of the way together.*
> —ERIC HARVEY AND STEVE VENTURA

> *People are illogical, unreasonable, and self-centered. Love them anyway.*
> —KENT M. KEITH

> *If you judge people you have no time to love them.*
> —MOTHER TERESA

DON'T LET ANGER GET OUT OF CONTROL

IT CAN WRECK RELATIONSHIPS AND RUIN LIVES

Old Testament Proverbs

A fool gives full vent to his anger.

—PROVERBS 29:11 NIV

A hot-tempered man must pay the penalty.

—PROVERBS 19:19 NIV

New Testament

But now you must rid yourselves of all such things as these: anger, rage, malice.

—COLOSSIANS 3:8 NIV

Any bitterness or bad temper or anger or shouting or abuse must be far removed from you—as must every kind of malice.

—EPHESIANS 4:31 JER

COMMANDMENT 5

DON'T LET ANGER GET OUT OF CONTROL
IT CAN WRECK RELATIONSHIPS AND RUIN LIVES

*Anyone can be angry. That is easy. But to be angry with
the right person, to the right degree, at the right time, for
the right purpose, and in the right way—that is not easy.*

—ARISTOTLE

WHAT THE SCRIPTURES SAY ABOUT ANGER

The Scriptures don't tell us we should never be angry. There
wasn't anyone in biblical times, and there isn't anyone now,
who hasn't felt justifiable anger on occasion. It's a natural emotion. In some cases, expressing our anger can have a positive result. Things like crime, injustice, discrimination, meanness,
rudeness, cheating, and lying make all of us angry. And our
anger can motivate us to correct something that's not right.
There's nothing wrong with this type of anger, and it's not con
demned in the Bible. The Scriptures don't tell us to eliminate
anger; they tell us to control it. Solomon refers to anger and
the problems it can cause several times in the Proverbs. He

warns us against being quick-tempered, hotheaded, and reckless. But in almost all cases, he suggests a solution as well: he recommends restraint, patience, self-control, wisdom, and prudence.

A fool shows his annoyance at once, but a prudent man overlooks an insult. (12:16 NIV)

A wise man fears the Lord and shuns evil, but a fool is hotheaded and reckless. (14:16 NIV)

A short-tempered man is a fool. He hates the man who is patient. (14:17 TLB)

A hot-tempered man stirs up dissension, but a patient man calms a quarrel. (15:18 NIV)

Only a fool flies into a rage. (20:3 JER)

A man without self-control is as defenseless as a city with broken-down walls. (25:28 TLB)

Mockers stir up a city, but wise men turn away anger. (29: 8 NIV)

The fool blurts out every angry feeling, but the wise subdues and restrains them. (29:11 JER)

A hot-tempered man starts fights and gets into all kinds of trouble. (29:22 TLB)

The message in the New Testament is essentially the same. It tells us to be patient, kind, and gentle so we can avoid the consequences of uncontrolled anger:

> *But when you follow your own wrong inclinations your lives will produce these evil results: . . . hatred and fighting, jealousy and anger.*
>
> —GALATIANS 5:19–20 TLB

> *Even if you are angry, do not sin: never let the sun set on your anger or else you will give the devil a foothold.*
>
> —EPHESIANS 4:26–27 JER

> *No more evil temper or furious rage . . .*
>
> —COLOSSIANS 3:8 PHI

> *Let every man be quick to listen but slow to use his tongue, and slow to lose his temper. For man's temper is never the means of achieving God's true goodness.*
>
> —JAMES 1:19–20 PHI

ANGER'S MANY FORMS

The dictionary not only helps us crystallize the meaning of a word, it increases our understanding of it by providing synonyms, explanations, and examples. The first definition of "anger" in *Merriam-Webster* is "a strong feeling of displeasure and usually of antagonism." The writers also point out that "anger" is a general term that "in itself conveys nothing about the intensity or justification or manifestation of the emotional state." So they provide us with a few additional terms that seem to illuminate the varieties of anger. Three of them are "rage," "fury," and "wrath." Here's what the dictionary says about them:

- **Rage:** "suggests loss of self-control from violence of emotion <screaming with *rage*>" Definition: "a violent and uncontrolled anger; a fit of violent wrath; insanity."

- **Fury:** "is overmastering destructive rage that can verge on madness <in her *fury* she accused everyone around her of betrayal>" Definition: "intense, disordered, and often destructive rage; frenzy."

- **Wrath:** "is likely to suggest a desire or intent to revenge or punish <rose in his *wrath* and struck his tormentor to the floor>" Definition: "strong vengeful anger or indignation."

PUTTING ANGER TO GOOD USE

There's nothing wrong with anger provided you use it constructively.

—WAYNE DYER

The American Psychological Association tells us that anger is a completely normal emotion. Everyone knows what it is, and everyone has felt it—either their own or someone else's. And it isn't always bad. When kept under control, it can often be a healthy emotion. But it can obviously lead to serious problems when it goes out of control. In 2003 Jack Nicholson and Adam Sandler starred in a movie called *Anger Management.* Though the fictitious characters in the movie are funny, the subject matter isn't. People who need anger management are in treatment because they're damaging other people's lives as well as their own. As the Scriptures tell us, a hot-tempered person "gets into all kinds of trouble."

Charles Spielberger, Ph.D., is a psychologist who specializes in the study of anger. He defines it as "an emotional state that varies in intensity from mild irritation to intense fury and rage." Like all other emotions, anger is accompanied by physiological changes. When we get angry, both our heart rate and our blood pressure go up. On the biochemical front, anger triggers the release of adrenaline and certain hormones.

The APA claims that one of the most common questions regarding anger is "Why are some people more angry than others?" Like other personality traits, the answer is complicated, but it is generally the result of the genes we inherit and the environment in which we grow up. Jerry Deffenbacher, Ph.D., another psychologist who specializes in anger management, says that some people really are more "hotheaded" than others. Because of their psychological makeup, they get angry more quickly and with much greater intensity than the average person does. There are other types who express their anger in a completely different way: instead of flying into a rage, they get grumpy and irritable. A third group simply withdraws and sulks.

A Word About My Own
Struggle with Anger

*Of the Seven Deadly Sins, anger is possibly the most fun.
To lick your wounds, to smack your lips over grievances long
past, to roll over your tongue the prospect of bitter
confrontations still to come, to savor to the last toothsome
morsel both the pain you are given and the pain you are
giving back—in many ways it is a feast for a king. The chief
drawback is that what you are wolfing down is yourself. The
skeleton at the feast is you.*

—Frederick Buechner

Back in the 1970s I don't think there was such a thing as
"anger management." If there had been, I would have been a
prime candidate for the treatment because I had a serious
problem controlling my anger. The pain and frustration of my
divorce seemed to trigger it, but I learned through counseling
that it was deep-seated. You may recall from an earlier chapter
my description of my father as an overwhelmingly negative
and angry person. As my counselor told me, "You have it in
your genes, and you grew up in an angry environment." Research has found that family background does play a big role in
producing hotheads. Unfortunately, that term was a good fit
for me for about ten years. I still remember the first time someone called me a "hothead." I angrily and loudly denied that I
was one—neatly proving his point.

It's difficult to write about this because it brings back so many painful memories of when I hurt others, including my sons, and damaged my own life. I didn't hit anyone or become violent, but I yelled a lot, just like my dad had done. I know it was painful to be on the receiving end of one of my tirades. I have indescribable remorse over them. It's a period in my life that I'd like forget, so I don't revisit it often. But I want to share it here in the hope it can help some of my readers. Countless numbers of people struggle with anger issues.

Because my books are in the prison library system, I receive a lot of letters from men who are incarcerated. Most of them have the same heartbreaking story to tell: they grew up in dysfunctional homes in which one or both parents were angry and abusive. That's where the pain and frustration began, and it was their inability to control the anger that had been passed on that eventually led to criminal acts, convictions, and prison.

I was more fortunate. My family background wasn't nearly as harsh as theirs. My father also had some admirable qualities, and my mother is the kindest and most loving person I've ever known. I was also privileged to have had a good education. It was because I'd studied psychology in college that I sought out counseling when my life seemed to be spinning out of control. It was an important decision, and the right one.

My counselor said something to me one day that changed everything. "Once you fully understand that your anger is both self-centered and self-destructive behavior," he assured me, "you'll want to do whatever's necessary to get it under control." I was stunned. I understood that uncontrolled anger leads to self-destructive behaviors because I'd already paid the price for some of my outbursts. But self-centered? What does frustration and anger have to do with self-centeredness? I was soon to learn that it has everything to do with self-centeredness. He asked me to tell him three things that made me angry. No problem. There were way more than three! I don't recall what my specific answers were, but I do remember his response. He said, "In other words, you get angry every time things don't go exactly the way you want them to."

He was right, of course, and he convinced me to focus on the truth of that statement, the root of the problem, rather than just the symptoms. He said that people who are easily angered have what psychologists call a "low tolerance for frustration." In other words, they don't take everyday annoyances, inconveniences, and other people's mistakes in stride as the average person does. They're overwhelmed by the sense that whatever it is shouldn't be happening to them; they've done nothing to deserve it. That explanation struck a chord in me. My anger was like that—I was mad when the world didn't deliver what I wanted and expected. It *was* self-centered. For the first time ever, I began to look at it and deal with it in a different manner.

My counselor made another important point in that same session. He knew I was a high school teacher, and he had a good understanding of the psychology of teenagers—raging hormones, rebelliousness, emotional outbursts, and all the other perks. "If you're having a problem controlling your anger, you must get mad at your students a lot," he surmised. I could truthfully say he was wrong there; I hardly ever showed my temper in the classroom. "Why do you think you control your anger at the high school so well, but not in other places?" he asked.

It seemed obvious to me: "Because my job is dealing with

teenagers. That's the way they are. I wouldn't be a very good teacher if I didn't know how to handle them." I could read the ah-ha look on his face. "Think about what you just said and apply it to life outside of your classroom. Other people are just being people—this is the way *they* are. If you can be patient and understanding with teenagers, you can be patient and understanding with anyone." Two major breakthroughs in one day!

> *Be not angry that you cannot make others as you wish them*
> *to be, since you cannot make yourself as you wish to be.*
> —THOMAS À KEMPIS

It wasn't long after that particular session with my counselor that I received some additional and invaluable help in dealing with my anger. Ten years of self-centered and shallow living left me feeling lonely and empty. My mentor asked me if I'd ever considered letting God back into my life. I said I'd been thinking about it for several weeks. He recommended a church, and I tried it the following Sunday. It was a highly emotional and deeply spiritual experience. There are no other words for it; I simply felt God calling me home. I met with the pastor the following Friday, and, after a long, tear-filled session, I returned to my faith.

One of the unexpected benefits of taking this step was the calm that came over me. I was astounded by it—I couldn't remember any time in my life in which I'd felt so peaceful. As I began to read the Scriptures, I understood the feeling better. King David wrote about it in his Psalms, and his son King Solomon wrote about it in his Proverbs:

Try to live in peace with everyone; work hard at it.

> —PSALM 34:14 TLB

For the good man—the blameless, the upright, the man of peace—he has a wonderful future ahead of him. For him there is a happy ending.

> —PSALM 37:37 TLB

A wise man controls his temper. He knows that anger causes mistakes. A relaxed attitude lengthens a man's life.

> —PROVERBS 14:29–30 TLB

In the New Testament we're told that the peace of God "transcends human understanding" (Philippians 4:7 PHI), and there are several more passages about our call to live peacefully:

Blessed are the peacemakers: they shall be recognized as children of God.

> —MATTHEW 5:9 JER

As far as your responsibility goes, live at peace with everyone.

> —ROMANS 12:18 PHI

But the fruit of the Spirit is love, joy, peace, patience, kindness, goodness, faithfulness, gentleness, and self-control.

> —GALATIANS 5:22 NIV

Live in peace with each other.

> —1 THESSALONIANS 5:13 NIV

Shortly after returning to my faith in the early 1980s, a friend who knew I struggled with hotheadedness gave me a Bible verse that has stuck in a powerful way. It remains in my thoughts daily. I recite it to myself whenever I'm tempted to become impatient and say or do something stupid, which, painful though it is to admit, is often. It's still a daily struggle, so drawing on this short, simple passage and repeating it to myself as a reminder have been the source of much comfort, peace, and strength. And it's helped keep me out of a lot of trouble.

> *Thou wilt keep him in perfect peace, whose mind is stayed on thee: because he trusteth in thee.*
>
> —ISAIAH 26:3 KJV

THE COST OF UNCONTROLLED ANGER

When anger arises, think of the consequences.

—CONFUCIUS

There's an old saying that reminds us, "Anger is only one letter short of danger." Both the writers of the Scriptures and modern-day psychologists would agree. They don't tell us to avoid anger, but they do tell us to learn to control it. Though it's a natural emotion, it can also be a harbinger of danger. Danger is defined by *Merriam-Webster* as "exposure or liability to injury, pain, harm, or loss." We can do all that and more when we allow our anger to develop into rage or fury. The reason I say *allow* is because it's always a choice. If we could follow the advice of Confucius in the quotation above, we could prevent a lot of damage—both to others and to ourselves.

When I was still in the classroom, I routinely asked both my teenage and adult students to give me feedback and their viewpoints on a variety of topics. They contributed in many ways to my previous books. The Dirty Thirty of offensive language in chapter 3 is just one example. While writing this chapter, I started thinking about all the horrible things that can result when a person lets his or her anger get out of control. Seeing a list of them might help some people realize just how deadly anger can be if it goes unchecked. I no longer have my students to help me out. But I do have some wonderful friends in the character education movement and have easy access to them through the wonder of e-mail. So I sent off a message to twenty of them and asked for some help.

The Ravages of Rage

How much more grievous are the consequences of anger than the causes of it.

—Marcus Aurelius

Here's my friends' list of the possible consequences of anger run amok:

1. The end of a life: Most murders are called "crimes of passion." Uncontrolled anger can also lead to suicide.

2. Battered children and battered wives: Anger often leads to physical abuse.

3. Rape: It's considered a crime of anger, power, and violence.

4. Injury: It can be the result of fighting another person in anger or hitting a stationary object out of frustration.

5. Destruction of property: It's often done as a means of revenge or as an act of aggression.

6. Threats: An enraged person can become a menace, putting someone else's life in peril.

7. Filthy language: Anger often leads to loud swearing and offensive words.

8. Verbal cruelty: Angry words can often hurt more than a fist, and they last longer.

9. Dysfunctional families: Children who grow up in an angry environment often develop serious social and emotional problems.

10. Divorce: Uncontrolled anger is a leading cause of the sky-high divorce rate.

11. Loss of friendship: Friends are eventually repelled by the toxic atmosphere created by frequent angry outbursts.

12. Damage to career: People have been stalled, demoted, and even fired due to anger management problems.

13. Damage to reputation: Constant anger can hurt a person professionally and socially.

14. Road rage: Anger can lead to accidents, property damage, injury, and lawsuits.

15. Physical ailments: High blood pressure, heart disease, trouble sleeping, strokes, and reduced blood flow to the brain are just a few.

16. Psychological problems: Depression, guilt, unhappiness, and loneliness can all stem from uncontrolled anger.

17. Intimidation: Angry people often control and bully others at home, at school, and in the workplace.

18. Legal problems: Excessive anger often leads to criminal acts, convictions, and incarceration.

19. Financial problems: Uncontrolled anger can result in people losing income from their jobs and often having to pay for damage they do.

20. Revenge: Seeking vengeance only nurtures anger and prolongs all its negative effects; the need to get even often leads to increased anger and greater problems.

21. Resentment: Carrying a grudge prevents a person from moving on to better things.

22. Irrational thinking: The angrier we get, the harder it is to reason and think clearly.

23. Blocks problem solving: Rage gives you tunnel vision; it's impossible to seek creative, peaceful resolutions while in a highly agitated state.

24. Prevents healing: A person who stays angry can never forgive or reconcile with friends and loved ones.

25. Lack of joy: When a person is angry, he or she can't have fun, be happy, know inner peace, or enjoy life.

Anger blows out the lamp of the mind.
—ROBERT GREEN INGERSOLL

Speak when you are angry—and you'll make the best speech you'll ever regret.
—DR. LAURENCE J. PETER

Whatever begins in anger ends in shame.
—BENJAMIN FRANKLIN

Holding on to anger is like grasping a hot coal with the intent of throwing it at someone else; you are the one who gets burned.

—BUDDHA

Anger, if not restrained, is frequently more hurtful to us than the injury that provokes it.

—SENECA

For every minute you are angry, you lose sixty seconds of happiness.

—RALPH WALDO EMERSON

PAIN, PENALTY, AND PROGRESS

A fool gives full vent to his anger, but a wise man keeps himself under control.

—PROVERBS 29:11 NIV

While writing this chapter I received a long and moving e-mail from a man who'd recently read my third book, *Choices That Change Lives*. He said he'd picked it up because he'd heard me talking on the radio about how I'd made mistakes in the past, learned from them, and then used my experiences to teach others. At the time he was going through something very difficult and painful that he'd brought upon himself, and he knew he needed to make some major changes. His biggest problem was his inability to control his temper. His wife couldn't take any more of his yelling and irrational outbursts and had decided to divorce him. She had urged him several times to get professional help, but he had refused. He thought he was "just a normal guy who gets mad like everyone else."

Now he knows differently. He wrote, "It has taken me a long time to understand, but I finally realized that my wife wants out because I have emotionally abused her for a long time. I have spent the last week mercilessly beating myself up." He said that one particular sentence in my book had a real impact on him and would ultimately help him heal and process his anger and unhappiness to become a better person. It reads, "Every day we wake up with the opportunity to become a better person than we were yesterday."

His poignant message ended on a positive note. He said he would do as I had done: "I will also seek help from professionals to help me get to the core of my pain." In closing he wrote, "I will eventually look at this dark time in my life as an opportunity to renew and to start the healing process." His story is a good example of how uncontrolled anger hurts others and destroys relationships. It also shows that there's always a price to pay when we don't learn to control our anger. As Solomon told us thousands of years ago, "A hot-tempered man must pay the penalty" (Proverbs 19:19 NIV).

There is hope in his story. Pain can be a great teacher. In addition, both our mistakes and our pain present us with some great opportunities. We can learn from our mistakes, and we can grow from them. Anger has been researched extensively in recent years, and the good news is that there are a number of ways in which it can be brought under control. The first step is admitting that there's a problem; the second is making a commitment to do something about it.

> *If you are patient in one moment of anger, you will escape a hundred days of sorrow.*
>
> —CHINESE PROVERB

HELP FOR HOTHEADS

Recognizing that there are different personality types, different types of anger, and different degrees of the problem, here are ten strategies that have proven valuable to a variety of people I know. For some, just one of these tools could be enough. Others might put a combination of two or more to work.

1. Count to ten—slowly. This is by far the oldest strategy in the book, and for a good reason—because it works. Thousands of years ago mothers were telling this to their kids. Now psychologists tell it to their patients with anger problems.

> *The greatest remedy for anger is delay.*
>
> —SENECA

> *When angry, count to ten before you speak; if very angry, a hundred.*
>
> —THOMAS JEFFERSON

2. Seek professional help. This should be the first step for people suffering from severe anger problems. Counselors, especially those who specialize in anger management, can be of immeasurable assistance in alleviating the pain.

3. Find an outlet. Many professionals advise people with pent-up aggression to find a way to release it in nondestructive ways. "Blowing off steam," whatever that means for you, can help. Strenuous physical exercise is commonly prescribed. Even a walk around the block to cool off and clear your head can work wonders.

4. Meditate. You don't have to be into New Age philosophy or be a disciple of the maharishi in order to try this. There are many types of meditation, and most of them are simple. Among the many physical and psychological benefits are slower heart rate, deeper sense of relaxation, decreased muscle tension, and reduction of anxiety. Yoga both stretches muscles and relaxes the mind.

5. Read. There are several good books on the subject of anger, its consequences, and how to manage the problem. Les Carter's *The Anger Trap* is outstanding. The subtitle is telling: "Free Yourself from the Frustrations That Sabotage Your Life."

6. Have an accountability partner. When a person is trying to overcome a destructive habit, it's always helpful to meet regularly with a group or an individual at least once a week. Knowing that you'll be held accountable on a regular basis provides motivation to work harder on the problem.

7. Pray. For believers who understand the true nature of prayer, it's a powerful source of strength and comfort. I have a friend who says this three-word prayer every time he feels anger coming on: "Come, Holy Spirit." He says it consistently works because he has faith that it will.

> *Everything you ask for in prayer, if you believe, if you have faith, you will receive.*
>
> —MATTHEW 21:22 PHI

8. Repeat a quotation or Bible verse. Many people have one or more of these memorized. When potential trouble pops up, they repeat the verse to themselves several times as a reminder to stay calm and get centered. For example, people with anger problems could repeat the quotations by Seneca or Jefferson above. A good Bible verse would be Proverbs 29:11 on page 113.

9. Learn to be patient. The emphasis here is on the word "learn." Patience doesn't come naturally to most people, especially Type As. But with commitment and hard work it *can* be learned. An excellent book on this subject is called *The Power of Patience* by M. J. Ryan.

10. Learn to forgive. This is essential for people who are prone to resentment. It poisons the mind and weighs a person down. Like patience, it can be learned. One of the best books ever written on the subject is *Forgive for Good* by Dr. Fred Luskin.

Holding on to anger, resentment and hurt only gives you tense muscles, a headache, and a sore jaw from clenching your teeth. Forgiveness gives you back the laughter and the lightness in your life.

—JOAN LUNDEN, IN *HEALTHY LIVING* MAGAZINE

Since Solomon was the master of common sense and wisdom, it's not surprising that he had much to say about controlling our anger. So much of the world's pain and suffering are caused by people who allow their anger to go unchecked. These people have never been taught how to take control of their emotions. Daniel Goleman, the author of the best-selling *Emotional Intelligence,* suggests that the reason so many teenagers and adults have anger problems is that we don't address it in our schools. He believes that good character, of which self-control is a significant part, can and should be taught to our children.

The bedrock of character is self-discipline; the virtuous life, as philosophers since Aristotle have observed, is based on self-control.

—DANIEL GOLEMAN

Your goodness must be accompanied by knowledge, your knowledge by self-control, your self-control by the ability to endure.

—2 PETER 2:6 PHI

PART II

FIVE THINGS
THE SCRIPTURES
TELL US TO DO

BECAUSE
THEY'RE GOOD FOR US

AN IMPORTANT PART of living a good life is learning to do the things that produce the best results. It takes a long time. When we're children, we're taught to share, to be respectful of others, to be helpful, and to be polite, as in saying "please" and "thank you." As we get older, we're told to have a good attitude, work hard, be fair and honest, and help those who are less fortunate. We're also encouraged to love others. We're told that our lives will be better if we do these things: we'll be happier, have more friends, and make the world a better place.

Long before our parents, teachers, pastors, and others began steering us onto the right path, the Scriptures were written. Boiled down to its most basic teaching, the Bible tells us that we reap what we sow. As discussed in part I, we're told that there are several things we should *not* do because we'll reap negative consequences—for others as well as for ourselves. But the Bible also gives us wonderful advice about some things we *should* do because we'll reap the benefits. When we do these things, we enrich the lives of others while enriching our own. This section of the book contains five of the essentials that will help us attain meaning and joy in our lives.

Prologue
The Root of All Our Virtues

IN THE PROLOGUE to part I, I fingered pride as the root of all our flaws. From it comes the ugliest stuff in our lives. It's the basic flaw with which we all come into the world. But there's more to us than that. We're also born with a couple of other characteristics that provide us with hope. First, we're born in "the image of God" and therefore capable of immeasurable good. Second, we're born with a free will, which means we always have the ability to choose to focus on either the positive or the negative elements of our nature.

If pride is at the heart of our weakness and vice, then humility, its opposite, is at the heart of our strengths and our virtues.

> *Humility leads to strength and not to weakness. It is the highest form of self-respect to admit mistakes and to make amends for them.*
>
> —JOHN JAY McCLOY

> *Humility, that low, sweet root,*
> *From which all heavenly virtues shoot.*
>
> —THOMAS MOORE

Virtue is defined on the Web site Wikipedia as "the moral excellence of a man or woman; . . . a virtue is a good character trait." But an even better definition can be found on The Virtues Project Web site. This is how six-year-old Janie explains it: "Virtues are what's good about us." There are literally hundreds of virtues, or positive character traits, and people could argue forever about which ones are most important. The truth is, they're all important, and the best thing is that there's nothing to stop us from claiming every one of them. We're born with the capacity to own and practice *all* of them.

TEN VIRTUES OF WHICH WE'RE ALL CAPABLE

Empathy	Patience	Forgiveness	Caring	Compassion
Giving	Honesty	Thankfulness	Love	Kindness

By anyone's standards, these are among the highest virtues we can attain. The Scriptures teach us that that humility is the foundation of all of them. In the Old Testament both David and Solomon advise and encourage us to develop humility, just as Jesus, Paul, and James do in the New Testament. All these great teachers point out the rewards of humility, wisdom chief among them.

He guides the humble in what is right and teaches them his way.

—PSALM 25:9 NIV

When pride comes, then comes disgrace, but with humility comes wisdom.

—Proverbs 11:2 NIV

For everyone who exalts himself will be humbled, and he who humbles himself will be exalted.

—Luke 14:11 NIV

Accept life with humility and patience, making allowances for each other because you love each other.

—Ephesians 4:2 PHI

Are there some wise and understanding men among you? Then your lives will be an example of the humility that is born of true wisdom.

—James 3:13 PHI

The great philosopher and theologian Saint Augustine says that none of the other virtues is possible unless we first have humility. He says, "In the soul in which this does not exist, there cannot be any other virtue except in mere appearance." It's the most difficult virtue to attain; yet it promises the greatest rewards—the other virtues.

COMMANDMENT 6

KEEP A POSITIVE OUTLOOK ON LIFE

IT'S THE FIRST STEP TOWARD JOY

Old Testament Proverb

The good man can look forward to happiness.

—PROVERBS 11:23 TLB

New Testament

Fix your minds on whatever is true and honourable and just and pure and lovely and praiseworthy.

—PHILIPPIANS 4:8 PHI

COMMANDMENT 6

KEEP A POSITIVE OUTLOOK ON LIFE
IT'S THE FIRST STEP TOWARD JOY

The cheerful heart has a continual feast.
—PROVERBS 15:15 NIV

For the joyous heart it is always festival time.
—PROVERBS 15:15 JER

When he is cheerful, everything seems right!
—PROVERBS 15:15 TLB

WHAT THE SCRIPTURES SAY ABOUT ATTITUDE

Throughout the Scriptures, from Genesis at the beginning of the Old Testament to Revelations at the end of the New Testament, there are literally hundreds of references to just about every kind of attitude human beings have ever adopted, both good and bad. We're advised to work on eliminating the attitudes that poison the soul and lead to problems and urged to work on developing attitudes that refresh and strengthen the soul and lead to joyful living. In the Old Testament, Solomon tells us that those who seek good will surely find it (Proverbs 11:27), while in the New Testament, Paul tells us to let the attitude of Jesus be our example (Philippians 1:5).

THE TRUE, GOOD, AND RIGHT

Fix your thoughts on what is true and good and right.
Think about things that are pure and lovely, and dwell on
the fine, good things in others.

—PHILIPPIANS 4:8 TLB

The Scriptures refer to more positive attitudes than to negative ones, again with the emphasis on consequences. A good attitude is the starting place for both *being* good and *doing* good. It's the engine that powers us in the right direction. A few examples: King David tells us to rejoice in each new day (Psalm 118:24), and Jesus tells us to be of good cheer (John 16:3). While there are far more than twenty positive attitudes mentioned in the Scriptures, the following are the ones most likely to reap the best results.

Humble	Happy	Peaceful	Encouraging
Forgiving	Kind	Hopeful	Confident
Cheerful	Gentle	Discerning	Calm
Patient	Thankful	Diligent	Gracious
Loving	Honest	Faithful	Sweet

BEING JOYFUL IS ATTITUDE NUMBER ONE

Joy, rather than happiness, is the goal of life, for joy is the emotion which accompanies our fulfilling our natures as human beings.

—ROLLO MAY

To be successful and happy, you need a positive attitude, an attitude of joy.

—KEITH HARRELL

The writers of the Bible would agree wholeheartedly with the psychologist Rollo May and the motivational speaker Keith Harrell. The word "joy" appears at least 155 times in the Old Testament and another 63 times in the New Testament. The word "rejoice" appears 32 times in the Old Testament and 18 times in the New Testament. There are few words that appear in the Scriptures as many times. I can only conclude that God wants us to be happy, positive, cheerful, and loving. In other words—joyful.

Although joy and happiness are related, they're not the same. For most of us, happiness is roughly equivalent to good fortune. In other words, it's determined by fortunate circumstances. We're happy when things are going well for us, when we get what we want, when we're having fun, when we win something, when we have good luck. It's the result of something good happening that's beyond our control. There's nothing wrong with happiness. We should treasure every moment of it. But it's fleeting, and no one can be happy all the time.

Joy is a feeling and an attitude of much greater depth. It comes from within, not from circumstances. It's a feeling of deep satisfaction with life. It's also an outlook on life that's closely related to thankfulness. Joyful people look at what's right with the world and with people instead of what's wrong. They have a special appreciation for all the good they see around them.

Of the countless great lessons I learned from my mom, the importance of being thankful was the most valuable. It's both an attitude and a habit. When I was younger I used to grouse, as all kids do, about the things I didn't have. My mom was there to gently remind me that I had more than most kids did. She showed me pictures in magazines of children who wore rags and lived in huts and shacks without electricity or plumbing. They lived without medical care and without the opportunity for an education. Sadly, this is still true in many parts of the world today. My mom's stories and pictures, and her tender way of reminding me to be thankful, left a deep and lasting impression on me. I was, indeed, fortunate, then as today. Her comment that "The happiest people in the world aren't the ones who *have* the most but the ones who are the most thankful for what they *do* have," was one that had staying power. I couldn't forget it if I wanted to, though of course I don't. Maybe this is why the word "thank" and variations of it appear in the Bible 29 times. We can't be joyful without being thankful.

> It is not how much we have, but how much we enjoy.
> —CHARLES SPURGEON

> Be thankful, whatever the circumstances may be.
> —THESSALONIANS 5:18 PHI

Another important thing to understand about joy is that it's the close companion of wisdom. Wise people look at life differently from the average person. They see the big picture, and they understand that there's far more good in the world than there is bad. They see more to be thankful about than to complain about. They accept life as it is and make the most of it in all circumstances instead of grumbling about the way things ought to be. They find joy both in little things and in grand achievements. They celebrate life. And wise people, regardless of their spiritual beliefs, agree with King David:

> *This is the day the Lord has made; let us be glad and rejoice in it.*
>
> —PSALM 118:24 NIV

As a Man Thinketh . . .

One of the most important factors in determining whether or not we'll have a positive outlook on life is our thinking process, or our self-talk. In the early 1900s a relatively unknown writer and philosopher in rural England wrote what might be called a long essay on the overwhelming power of mind-set. His name was James Allen, and his little booklet has become a classic. It's called *As a Man Thinketh*. Allen was born in 1864 and died suddenly at age forty-eight in 1912. Although he wrote other books that were deeply philosophical and spiritual, this short work is the one that's influenced millions of people, including many of the great thinkers of modern times. Thousands of people, including this author, read his book at least once a year. The title comes from a verse in the King James translation of the Bible:

As a man thinketh in his heart, so is he.

—PROVERBS 23:7

Allen had only the King James version available to him. And he used that one simple verse to teach us better than anyone before or after him the power of thought, the importance of attitude. Our outlook on life is determined by what goes on inside our heads. As Allen says, the mind is the "masterweaver." It shapes two critically important aspects of life: our character and our circumstances. The mind operates as a control center; it points the way, and it chooses the path. The thoughts that occupy our minds eventually mold our character—the type of person we become. They also influence our circumstances more than most people realize. The mind has a way of attracting that which it thinks about.

Allen writes that one becomes a person of integrity and solid character as the result of "continued effort in right thinking." Conversely, a person develops poor character as a result of the "continued harboring of groveling thoughts."

A cheerful heart is good medicine, but a crushed spirit dries up the bones.

—PROVERBS 17:22 NIV

*A good man produces good things from the good stored up
in his heart, and a bad man produces evil things from his
own stores of evil.*

—LUKE 6:45

We live in a society in which people constantly complain
that they're the victims of circumstances—from bad genes to
bad luck, from a bad childhood to a bad job market. To those
with a victim mentality, those who are doing well are "just
lucky." James Allen would be shaking his head. He would say
that as long as they continue to think that way, their lives will
stay the same. When they change their thinking, as millions
have done before them, their circumstances will also change.
Allen wrote that we are the masters of our thoughts and therefore the makers of "condition, environment, and destiny."

*The people who get on in this world are the people who get
up and look for the circumstances they want, and, if they
can't find them, make them.*

—GEORGE BERNARD SHAW

*Ask, and it will be given to you; seek and you will find;
knock and the door will be opened to you.*

—MATTHEW 7:7 NIV

Allen uses some vivid analogies to describe the mind and
how it operates. He first compares it to a mine: before we can
find either gold or diamonds, we have to first search for a vein

and then dig far beneath the surface. In order to find the riches within our minds, we must do the same things—search and dig. He says, "Man can find every truth connected with his being if he will dig deep into the mine of his soul." Popular culture makes this especially challenging today, as the mighty advertising industry urges us to do just the opposite. It doesn't want us to dig, and marketers don't want us to think for ourselves. Advertising bombards us daily with surface-level messages about the things we should have to look good or feel good. Don't think—buy! But if we want to find the treasure inside us, we need to be willing to do some digging.

Another analogy Allen uses to describe the mind is a garden. We sow a healthy garden with good seeds and fertile soil. It then requires constant care through feeding and weeding. The good seeds are ideas and knowledge. The fertile soil is an open mind. The feeding is study and contemplation, and the weeding consists of pulling out negative thoughts. Allen says that the garden "may be intelligently cultivated or allowed to run wild; but whether cultivated or neglected, it must, and will, bring forth."

> Just as the gardener cultivates his plot, keeping it free from weeds, and growing the flowers and fruits which he requires, so may a man tend the garden of his mind, weeding out all the wrong, useless, and impure thoughts, and cultivating toward perfection the flowers and fruits of right, useful, and pure thoughts. By pursuing this process, a man sooner or later discovers that he is the master-gardener of his soul, the director of his life.
>
> —JAMES ALLEN

The reaping and sowing we do in life begin with our attitude. The Scriptures tell us that in order to reap a good life, we need to have a positive outlook and believe that it's possible. They tell us to be thankful and joyful, and above all to have hope. Allen tells us that all of this is possible if we learn how to manage and control our thoughts:

> The outer world of circumstance shapes itself to the inner world of thought, and both pleasant and unpleasant external conditions are factors which make for the ultimate good of the individual. As the reaper of his own harvest, man learns both by suffering and bliss.
>
> Circumstance does not make the man; it reveals him to himself.
>
> Not what he wishes and prays for does man get, but what he justly earns. His wishes and prayers are only gratified and answered when they harmonize with his thoughts and actions.
>
> Good thoughts and actions can never produce bad results; bad thoughts and actions can never produce good results.
>
> A man only begins to be a man when he ceases to whine and revile, and commences to search for the hidden justice which regulates his life.
>
> To think well of all, to be cheerful with all, to patiently learn to find the good in all—such unselfish thoughts are the very portals of heaven.
>
> —JAMES ALLEN

Does God Want Us to Be Positive Thinkers?

Everything is possible for him who believes.

—MARK 9:23 NIV

More than fifty years ago a Protestant minister wrote what became one of the best-selling books of all time. It has sold more than 20 million copies in more than forty languages. It continues to sell well today, and millions of people claim that reading it has changed their lives. The book is *The Power of Positive Thinking,* and the author is Norman Vincent Peale (1898–1993).

Though Peale was an ordained minister and his book has been a boon to millions, he's been severely criticized in some Protestant circles. Among other things, Peale was accused of being a liberal, an advocate of New Age philosophy, a disciple of self-esteem, and a motivational speaker who preferred pop psychology to the word of God.

I bring up his disputed status because not everyone believes that positive thinking is taught in the Scriptures. In fact, many people believe that positive thinking stands in direct opposition to the teachings of the Scriptures because it encourages people to rely on themselves and their own powers rather than God. I'm not enough of an expert on the Bible to say whether Peale was or was not perfectly in line with its teachings, but there's no arguing with the fact that Peale mentions God, urges prayer, and cites Scripture throughout the book. In the end I think the controversy is silly. Once again, these voices of opposition come from self-righteous, judgmental fundamentalists who claim that their interpretation of the Scriptures is the only one.

I read the book many years ago, when I was angry and full of negative thoughts. I was convinced that life had dealt me a bad hand. Did the book help? Absolutely. It helped me realize that God gave me a brain along with free will to use it how I chose. I was using it poorly at the time, and Peale's book, along with Allen's and a few others, got me to think differently and better. I don't think God wants us to be gloomy, negative, angry, judgmental, or condemning. Common sense tells us that those kinds of attitudes are counterproductive. And they're in direct opposition to the teachings of the Scriptures. David told us to rejoice, Solomon told us to seek the good, Jesus told us to be cheerful, and Paul told us to concentrate our thoughts on the good things in life.

He who seeks good finds goodwill.

—PROVERBS 11:27 NIV

ATTITUDE IS A CHOICE

I have set before you life or death, blessing or curse. Oh, that you would choose life; that you and your children might live!

—DEUTERONOMY 30:19 TLB

*Everything can be taken from a man but one thing, the last
of the human freedoms—to choose one's attitude in any
given set of circumstances, to choose one's own way.*

—Viktor Frankl

In the two previous sections I discussed books that helped me better understand the power of thought and the importance of attitude. Here I'll focus on a third—another classic that's changed countless lives, mine among them. The book is *Man's Search for Meaning* by Viktor Frankl (1905–1997). I've written about it before, but I'm writing about it again for a couple of reasons. One, I'm a teacher and can never resist the opportunity to reinforce an important point, and this is a critically important point. Two, Frankl's book is always in the forefront of my mind. I reread parts of it every year and remind myself a few times every day that I'm always free to choose my attitude no matter what's going on around me. I spent many years teaching this concept to my students, both kids and adults, and I still do whenever I have the chance.

In case you're unfamiliar with the book, it was published in the United States in 1959 and tells the story of the time the author spent in a concentration camp during World War II. Frankl was a young Jewish physician in Vienna during the Nazi regime. Shortly after his marriage in 1942, he and his wife, parents, and brother were sent to Nazi concentration camps. He spent the next three years at Auschwitz and three other camps. He was the only member of his family to survive. In the first section of the book, he describes the atrocious and inhuman suffering that he and his fellow prisoners were subjected to.

In those three years Frankl lost everything that mattered to him—his wife and other family members, his home, all his earthly possessions, and his medical practice. He writes that one day while he was waiting for the shower he suddenly became aware of how truly naked he was. "We really had nothing now except our bare bodies—even minus hair; all we possessed, literally, was our naked existence." The Nazis had taken virtually everything away from him and his fellow inmates, many of whom eventually lost the will to live. But as Frankl discovered, he and others who drew upon their inner resources managed to survive.

Two of those inner resources were imagination and hope. Frankl and others survived by envisioning their futures. They believed they would someday be freed and would go on to live happy and productive lives. The more specific their plans for the future, the more hope they had. They realized that no matter what the Nazis did to them, they were still free to choose their own thoughts, their own hopes for the future, and their own attitudes, no matter how atrocious their immediate circumstances. This is why Frankl calls it the last of human freedoms.

The fact that we're free to choose our own thoughts and attitudes, no matter how bad things look, is a simple yet profound concept. Grasping this concept can be life-changing, yet many people are totally unaware of it. When I ask people what determines their attitudes, here's what I most often hear in response:

- "The mood I'm in"
- "The day of the week"
- "Where I am"

- "How much sleep I got last night"
- "Who I'm with"
- "What I'm doing"
- "How I'm being treated"
- "How the planets are lined up"
- "Whatever"

The millions of people who think this way will live their entire lives disconnected from their greatest power—the power to choose their own attitudes regardless of the circumstances. People, things, and events outside themselves will always determine their destiny. How liberating it is to discover that we have control over our lives because we have control over our thoughts!

> *A man can only rise, conquer, and achieve by lifting his thoughts.*
>
> —JAMES ALLEN

> *The greatest discovery of my generation is that a human being can alter his life by altering his attitudes of mind.*
>
> —WILLIAM JAMES

NASTY ATTITUDES THE SCRIPTURES URGE US TO AVOID

Do all you have to do without grumbling.

—PHILIPPIANS 2:14 PHI

Although the emphasis in this chapter is on positive attitudes written about in the Scriptures, it might be helpful to take a brief look at the negative attitudes we're better off without. There are far more than twenty, but these are the most potent. We'd do well to follow the advice of the great teachers in the Bible and avoid them, because leaving them behind is actually one of the most positive things you can do.

Selfish	Vengeful	Greedy	Proud
Bitter	Downcast	Despairing	Angry
Jealous	Haughty	Deceitful	Conceited
Gloomy	Divisive	Vain	Disobedient
Judgmental	Arrogant	Hateful	Disrespectful

A RABBI AND A PREACHER ON THE IMPORTANCE OF ATTITUDE

Rabbi Harold Kushner and Chuck Swindoll are well-known religious leaders who've touched the hearts of people of their faiths. But what makes them particularly effective writers and speakers is that their words also comfort and inspire people of different faiths and even those with no particular faith at all. Both have written extensively about the importance of attitude.

Rabbi Kushner became well known in the early 1980s with the publication of his best-selling book *When Bad Things Happen to Good People.* It helped literally millions of people deal with their pain, no matter what kind of pain it was. Kushner himself had suffered great pain through the fourteen-year illness and eventual death of his son Aaron. He described himself as a man who had been "hurt by life." But instead of wallowing in self-pity, he found meaning in his suffering and learned to deal with his loss. I, for one, am grateful he decided to share his story, first with his congregation and then with the world. His story has always reminded me of that of Viktor Frankl. Both men suffered deeply and unfairly. Both men realized they had a choice to make—to wallow in their suffering or to embrace hope. And both men used their pain to help others.

Rabbi Kushner didn't advise us about what to do *if* bad things happen, and he didn't try to explain *why* bad things happen. He offered us help for *when* bad things happen. Because one of the realities of life is that bad things *do* happen—to both good and bad people. We all face adversity, pain, and loss in our lives. The question is, how are we going to deal with it?

Kushner writes at great length about the story of Job in the Old Testament. He says, "The Book of Job is probably the greatest, fullest, most profound discussion of the subject of good people suffering ever written." Poor Job suffered every kind of loss possible over a period of many years. But he managed to endure because he didn't give up and because he searched for meaning in his suffering. Kushner says this story teaches us not to let undeserved misfortune and pain destroy us but to grow from it.

Rabbi Kushner advises us to move away from the question "Why did this happen to me?" and instead ask, "Now that this has happened, what shall I do about it?" He answers this question at the end of the book. He says God gives us the ability to forgive and to love, and if we use them we can "live fully, bravely, and meaningfully in this less-than-perfect world."

Pain is inevitable. Misery is optional.

—TIM HANSEL

Chuck Swindoll is an evangelical Christian pastor, educator, and radio preacher. He's well known as the author of more than fifty books and for his radio show *Insight for Living*, which is broadcast on both Christian and non-Christian stations. Although he has his critics within the Christian community (who doesn't?), he appeals to people of all beliefs and has millions of followers. His hopeful message is down to earth, easy to understand, and full of common sense.

Swindoll talks and writes about the importance of attitude from both biblical and psychological viewpoints. He says the most important decision he makes on a day-to-day basis is his choice of attitude. Attitude, he says, is the thing that "keeps me going or cripples my progress."

Swindoll wrote one of the most powerful statements on the importance of attitude I've ever read. It's so well known, it's been printed on cards and posters and quoted in print and online countless times. I kept a large poster of it in my classroom for many years to remind my students (and myself!) that attitude is always a choice, the most important one we make every day of our lives. Here's his wisdom:

> *The longer I live, the more I realize the impact of attitude on life. Attitude, to me, is more important than facts. It is more important than the past, than education, than money, than circumstances, than failures, than successes, than what other people think or say or do. It is more important than appearance, giftedness, or skill. It will make or break a*

*company . . . . a church . . . a home. The remarkable thing is
we have a choice every day regarding the attitude we will
embrace for that day. We cannot change the inevitable. The
only thing we can do is play on the one string we have, and
that is our attitude. I am convinced that life is 10% what
happens to me, and 90% how I react to it. And so it is with
you . . . we are in charge of our attitudes.*

—CHUCK SWINDOLL

Moses, Job, David, Solomon, Jesus, Paul, and James would
agree. The first step toward finding the joy the Scriptures
promise us is developing a positive outlook on life.

*You turned my wailing into dancing; you removed my sack-
cloth and clothed me with joy.*

—PSALM 30:11 NIV

COMMANDMENT 7

BRING OUT THE BEST IN OTHER PEOPLE

IT'S BETTER TO BUILD UP THAN TO TEAR DOWN

Old Testament Proverbs

As iron sharpens iron, so one sharpens another.

—PROVERBS 17:27 NIV

A word aptly spoken is like apples of gold in settings of silver.

—PROVERBS 25:11 NIV

New Testament

Let your words be for the improvement of others, as occasion offers.

—EPHESIANS 4:29 JER

Therefore encourage one another and build each other up.

—1 THESSALONIANS 5:11 NIV

COMMANDMENT 7

BRING OUT THE BEST IN OTHER PEOPLE

IT'S BETTER TO BUILD UP THAN TO TEAR DOWN

The mouth of the upright is a life-giving fountain.
— PROVERBS 10:11 JER

Say only what is good and helpful to those you are talking to, and what will give them a blessing.
— EPHESIANS 4:29 TLB

ON BEING A LIFE-ENHANCER

Throughout both the Old and New Testaments we're reminded that we can have enormous influence on the people with whom we come into contact. That influence can be for good or for bad. As Solomon says, the tongue has the power of life or death (Proverbs 18:21). Chapter 3 was about the damage we can cause with destructive language. This chapter focuses on the good we can do when we use kind and affirming language.

What's the best thing you could ever say about another person? That she's caring? That he's loving? Conscientious? Principled? Courageous? Giving? Strong? Dependable? Honest? There are a lot of positive words we can use to describe the people we admire. For many years I've used a simple phrase to describe these kinds of people. I call them life-enhancers, people who improve, strengthen, and beautify the world around them. In their interactions with other people, they bring out the best in everyone. We've all been blessed by these types of people. They see something good in us, and then they help us see it too. More important, they help us tap into it. They enhance our lives.

Would anyone call you a life-enhancer? Do you show genuine interest in other people? Do you express concern for them? Do you look for the good in them? Do you help them see it? Do you acknowledge people when they do something well? Do you express your appreciation for them? Do you build on their strengths? Do you encourage them? These are some of the many ways in which we can bring out the best in other people. They're exactly what the authors of the Scriptures tell us we should be doing.

The lips of the righteous nourish many.
                                     —Proverbs 10:21 NIV

Life-enhancers are people who make us glad we're alive. When we're down, they lift us up. When we're hurting, they comfort us. When we're discouraged, they give us hope. When we do something well, they celebrate with us. When we need help, they offer it. When we get off track, they help us find our way back. When we lack experience, they teach us. When we're kind, they make us feel appreciated. When we see the bad, they help us see the good. When we're about to give up, they give us hope. Even when life is good, they make it better. They enhance it.

WHAT ALL GOOD LEADERS DO

What are the primary responsibilities of the people who hold the following positions?

- Parent
- Teacher
- Coach
- Rabbi/pastor
- Mentor
- Business leader
- Elected official
- Military leader
- Head of a service organization

I've put that question to hundreds of audiences: kids of all ages, adults of all ages, people in a wide variety of professions, people of different faiths, people of different political viewpoints. Regardless of their stage or position in life, their answers are remarkably similar. Here are the four I hear the most often:

1. "To get the job done."
2. "To get people to produce."
3. "To teach people how to do things right."
4. "To delegate authority."

All these are true—good leaders do delegate, teach, get people to produce, and ultimately get the job done. But there's a simpler answer that covers all that ground. It is "To bring out the best in the people you're leading." If a mother sees the good in her daughter, taps into it, and encourages the child to become her best, she's a good leader. If a CEO sees the good in an employee, taps into it, and encourages the worker to become his best, he's a good leader. You see where I'm going with this. The job gets done when the person in charge brings out the best in the people he or she is leading.

Paradoxically, the most effective way to bring out the best in others is to serve them. Since we so often think of a leader as a hard charging, forceful, take-no-prisoners type, the idea of leader as servant may seem misguided. Yet it's been proven over and over, from biblical times to the present, that the servant leader can be as effective as any other type of leader. In fact, in many situations the servant leader is the only one who will succeed.

What is a servant leader? According to the man who coined the term, Robert K. Greenleaf, a servant leader is one who chooses to serve others first and then lead: "Servant leadership encourages collaboration, trust, foresight, listening, and the ethical use of power and empowerment." That's an excerpt from Greenleaf's 1970 essay "The Servant as Leader." In it he distinguishes between the leader-first and servant-first types of leaders. He calls them "two extreme types." Greenleaf says, "The difference manifests itself in the care taken by the servant-first to make sure that other people's highest priority needs are being served."

On the Leadersdirect Web site, servant leadership is explained this way: "The essential idea is that the leader serves the people he/she leads which implies that they are an end in themselves rather than a means to an organizational purpose or bottom line." The site also answers the question "What do servant leaders do?"

- Devote themselves to serving the needs of organization members.
- Develop employees to bring out the best in them.
- Coach others and encourage their self-expression.
- Facilitate personal growth in all who work with them.
- Listen and build a sense of community.

Although "servant leader" was originated as a business concept, it's easy to see how the same principles can apply at home, in the classroom, on the athletic field, in a place of worship, or in any other institution. If we substitute the word "people" for the word "employees" in the list above, we see that all the principles can be applied to a servant leader no matter where he or she is. And though Greenleaf originated the term in 1970, servant leaders have been around for thousands of years. In the Old Testament, people like Abraham, Moses, Joseph, and David are among the great servant leaders. Each was effective because he loved and cared for the people he led. In the New Testament we see Jesus as the ultimate servant leader, and his example was followed by Paul, John the Baptist, and Peter.

We've had no shortage of servant leaders in recent history. A few who stand out are Albert Schweitzer; Mahatma Gandhi; Nelson Mandela; Martin Luther King, Jr.; Mother Teresa; Ronald Reagan; Billy Graham; Jimmy Carter; John Paul II; and the Dalai Lama. In the world of business, HP's David Packard was the prototype of the servant leader, while in the world of sports no one has been a better example than basketball coach John Wooden. There have been countless other lesser-known, highly effective servant leaders—you might know one or more yourself. Although some people have criticized servant leadership as "too religious" and others have called it a gimmick, the record of history proves that it works.

Whoever wants to become great must become a servant.
—MATTHEW 20:27 MES

THE GREATEST SERVANT LEADER THIS SIDE OF THE BIBLE

More books have been written about Abraham Lincoln than any other American. And no one in this country has received more praise. So many things have been named in Lincoln's honor, it would be impossible to list them all here. There's a good reason: he was arguably the greatest American who ever lived. Leo Tolstoy, the brilliant Russian historian, said of Lincoln, "The greatness of Napoleon, Caesar, or Washington is only moonlight by the sun of Lincoln. His example is universal and will last thousands of years. . . . He was bigger than his country—bigger than all the presidents together . . . and as a great character he will live as long as the world lives." John Hay, who served as Lincoln's personal assistant in the White House and later as secretary of state under two presidents, called Lincoln "the greatest character since Christ."

What made Lincoln so great? He was a servant leader. He brought out the best in the people around him. I first recognized this truth as a history major in college. My favorite professor was Dr. Ashbrook Lincoln. He taught U.S. History in a way that fascinated me and had a great influence on my own teaching career. His overriding belief was that "People make history," so he taught the history of our country through biography. Most of his lectures were the life stories of great people like Benjamin Franklin, Thomas Jefferson, George Washington, John Marshall, Andrew Jackson, and others who forged our nation. Among his favorite presidents were Theodore Roosevelt and Harry Truman, but number one was clearly Abraham Lincoln.

His colleagues in the history department affectionately called Dr. Lincoln "Abe," and he signed his name "A. Lincoln." His students often asked if he was the great-grandson of President Lincoln. He wasn't, but said that even if his name were Smith, he'd feel the same about our greatest president. More than forty years later, I have vivid memories of Dr. Lincoln's many lectures, stories, and anecdotes about President Lincoln. He convinced me that Leo Tolstoy and John Hay were right.

One of my fellow history majors asked Dr. Lincoln one day what Lincoln's greatest characteristic had been. Without a second's hesitation he answered, "His ability to bring out the best in other people, especially among those with whom he worked in the White House." He went on to describe the personalities and enormous egos of the men in Lincoln's cabinet. Several of them had contested Lincoln for the presidency, and each considered himself superior to the president in both intellect and ability.

Because they had been political rivals and harsh critics, Lincoln could have shut them out after winning the presidency. That's what most politicians do. But he did just the opposite: he recognized their talents and knew they had something of value to offer, so he asked them to serve their country during a time of great crisis—the Civil War. Lincoln was not only the greatest president but also the most humble. He didn't care who got the credit. He just wanted to serve his country. And in doing that, he served the diverse group of men in his cabinet. He pointed out their strengths, told them he and the country needed them, and thanked and praised them often. He brought out the best in them.

No one has captured the genius of Lincoln better than the Pulitzer Prize–winning historian Doris Kearns Goodwin. Her 2005 book, *Team of Rivals,* the result of ten years of research, captures the essence of Lincoln's humility, integrity, empathy, and servant leadership. It's rare when a 900-page, thirty-five-dollar history book hits the best-seller lists, but this one did. It's a classic on leadership and well worth the money and the time it takes to read.

Kearns points out at the beginning of the book that "Every member of this administration was better known, better educated, and more experienced in public life than Lincoln. . . . It soon became clear, however, that Abraham Lincoln would emerge the undisputed captain of this most unusual cabinet, truly a team of rivals." She says that his real genius was revealed "through his extraordinary array of personal qualities that enabled him to form friendships with men who had previously opposed him; to repair injured feelings that, left untended, might have escalated into permanent hostility; to assume responsibility for the failures of subordinates; to share credit with ease; and to learn from mistakes." Kearns says that Lincoln's greatest qualities were "kindness, sensitivity, compassion, honesty, and empathy." How I wish every person in public office in this country would read Kearns's book and learn what it means to be a servant leader.

> *Anyone wanting to be a leader among you must be your servant.*
>
> —Matthew 20:26 TLB

Seven Ways to Bring Out the Best in Other People

> *Strength is for service, not status. Each of us needs to look after the good of the people around us, asking ourselves, "How can I help?"*
>
> —Romans 15:2 MES

This book would be way too long if I included all the suggestions contained in the Scriptures for bringing out the best in others. So I've zeroed in on some of the basics, the ones we have the opportunity to do on an almost daily basis. Here are seven ways in which we can enhance the lives of those around us:

1. Show genuine interest.
2. Listen with your heart.
3. Teach and mentor.

4. Affirm and praise.
5. Encourage and inspire.
6. Be a source of comfort.
7. Celebrate life!

1. Show genuine interest

Don't become snobbish but take a real interest in ordinary people.

—ROMANS 12:16 PHI

We're all aware that there's a serious hunger crisis in the world. Thousands of people die every day from malnutrition. As tragic as this is, there's another kind of hunger that's also destroying people's lives. It extends far beyond the third world—to every country, in fact—and it's especially heartbreaking in the United States. It's the hunger for attention. Not the need to be the center of attention or become famous, but the need to be recognized as a human being. Next to our physical needs of water, air, food, and safety, it's an absolute essential for both survival and growth. Yet, millions of people go to bed every night feeling as if they don't matter. Much of the problem could be solved with simple acts of kindness—acknowledging other people, letting them know that they count.

In the Old Testament, Solomon tells us to not become haughty, to not place ourselves above others. Other leaders in the Bible urge us to pay heed to the needs of those around us. In the New Testament, Jesus tells us to treat everyone as we would like to be treated under the same circumstances. And Paul tells us to take a genuine interest in all types of people. Unfortunately, this happens only rarely. We pay a lot of attention to celebrities, people with power and acclaim, people who can give us a leg up, and people who are like us, but rarely do we go out of our way to pay attention to the types of people who need it the most.

We so often treat the "little people"—those in low-paying service jobs—as if they're nonpersons. Here's an example; I see it happen more than forty times year. When I fly to speaking engagements, I park my car at one of those "park and fly" places near the San Francisco airport. The shuttle bus drivers, usually immigrants who haven't been in the country long, pick me up at my car, say a friendly hello, help me get my bags onto the bus, drive me to the airport, and then help me get my bags off the bus. While I greatly appreciate their help, it saddens me to see how often these hardworking people are treated poorly. The overwhelming majority of travelers who use the shuttle service don't acknowledge the driver's greeting, make eye contact, or say thanks for the help with the bags, and rarely give them a tip.

This is but one of millions of stories that occur on a daily basis. We all agree with the Golden Rule in principle, but we don't always put it into practice. A few months before writing this book, I read an article in the *San Francisco Chronicle* written by a psychologist. It was about the type of people who are most ignored—the poor, the elderly, the disabled, and minorities, especially if they happen to hold a low-paying job. The writer cited Abraham Maslow's well-known Hierarchy of Needs Theory. It was Maslow's belief that a person can't progress in life unless basic needs are met first. One of those needs is a sense of belonging. When it isn't met, people feel insignificant and alienated. The author suggested that we could add much joy to the lives of such people with some simple acts of kindness—eye contact, a smile, a greeting, a question, a thank-you. He ended his article with this quotation:

> *A great man shows his greatness by the way he treats little men.*
>
> —THOMAS CARLYLE

2. Listen with your heart

> *He who holds his tongue is wise.*
>
> —PROVERBS 10:19 NIV

> *Let the wise listen and learn yet more.*
>
> —PROVERBS 1:5 JER

Most of this chapter is about using language that has a positive effect on others. But we can acknowledge others positively without ever opening our mouths—by listening. It's a skill, and, like any skill, it's developed through hard work and practice, practice, practice. Many schools and colleges offer speech courses, but precious few offer a course in listening. Most people think hearing and listening are the same. They're not. We hear with our ears; it's a physiological function. We listen with our hearts; it's a social, psychological, and emotional function.

During a recent trip to Singapore I spoke about how important listening is to effective communication. In my talk I quoted an ancient Greek philosopher:

We have two ears and one mouth so that we can listen twice as much as we speak.

—EPICTETUS

In that same talk I referred to the theory of Alan Loy McGinnis, a family therapist and author. He says, "Good listeners listen with their eyes." When someone is talking to us, our eyes will let him or her know whether we're *really* listening. When we look into the other person's eyes, we're sending a message, namely, "What you have to say is important. I'm giving you my full attention." Finally, I mentioned that good listening takes empathy and concentration, and that it's hard work. We listen with our total being, including our core—the heart.

Shortly after my talk, a Chinese man came up to me and asked if I had ever seen the symbol for "listen" in his language. He assumed from the nature of my talk that I had. I told him no, so he drew it for me. It had several parts, each relating to the various aspects of listening. One of the symbols represents the mouth, while another represents the ears. The most interesting part was a symbol for ten eyes. One mouth, two ears, and ten eyes. He explained that there were ten eyes because they're so important in communicating to the other person that we're really listening. At the center of the symbol are a *one* and a *heart.* In other words, all the parts that lead to genuine listening add up to a single thing—the heart.

"Be careful how you listen," he said to them.

—MARK 4:24 PHI

3. Teach and mentor

The teaching of the wise is a fountain of life.
—PROVERBS 13:14 NIV

Nothing helps bring out the best in us like teaching and mentoring. Although classroom teaching at all levels can be of great value, I'm referring here to another type of teaching. We're all teachers. Almost every day of our lives we come into contact with people who can benefit from our knowledge and experience. We have a sacred obligation to help others learn new skills and to develop a greater understanding of how life works. At the same time, we regularly come into contact with people who know something we don't know, have a skill we don't have, and understand some aspect of life better than we do. We're all teachers, and we're all learners. And we bring out the best in one another when we share our knowledge and wisdom.

In my book *Choices That Change Lives,* I urged people to find a good mentor, or two, or more. They're out there, they're available to us, and each of them can enrich our lives. While I still feel strongly that we should all have mentors, I'm suggesting something different here—*that you be* a mentor.

We can have mentors and be mentors at the same time. Over a period of many years, I've been mentored in teaching, speaking, writing, photography, gardening, athletics, technology, and, most important, matters of faith. There's a double blessing here. My mentors have helped me develop skills and increase in knowledge and understanding of different aspects of life. That's the first blessing. The second blessing is being able to pass on to others what I've learned—except when it comes to operating a computer. No one is ever going to seek me out for that.

Teaching and mentoring are always win-win. There are excitement and joy in learning something new or going deeper. And there are equal excitement and joy in passing them on to others. One of the main goals of life is ongoing learning and growth, and there's scientific evidence that such a thing is more than possible—it's what our brains crave. Researchers have been accumulating more and more evidence that human brain development is a lifelong process—it doesn't stop when we reach adulthood and then plateau. And, as the Scriptures tell us, we can enhance the lives of others while enhancing our own.

The wise man is known for his common sense, and a pleasant teacher is the best.

—PROVERBS 16:21 TLB

The wise in heart are called discerning, and pleasant words promote instruction.

—PROVERBS 16:21 NIV

4. Affirm and praise

Do not withhold good from those who deserve it, when it is in your power to act.

—PROVERBS 3:27 NIV

Do not let any unwholesome talk come out of your mouths,
but only what is helpful for building others up according to
their needs, that it may benefit those who listen.

—EPHESIANS 4:29 NIV

My second book, *Positive Words, Powerful Results,* is about the impact our words can have. I wrote it for two simple reasons: first, to remind people that we tend to take language for granted and are often oblivious to the impact our words can have; second, to urge people to choose their words more carefully, especially those that affirm life in others.

The words "affirm" and "praise" are two of the most powerful in our language. They mean finding the good in other people and telling them what you have found. They mean being nurturing and supportive. They mean acknowledging others when they do something well. They mean building on people's strengths. In his classic book *How to Win Friends and Influence People,* Dale Carnegie says, "Give the other person a good reputation to live up to." We do that when we catch people doing things right. No one is ever too young or too old to bask in another's praise, so try it. When you see your son, daughter, friend, or parent do well, let them know.

We increase whatever we praise. The whole creation
responds to praise, and is glad.

—CHARLES FILLMORE

5. Encourage and inspire

*So give encouragement to each other, and keep
strengthening one another.*

—THESSALONIANS 5:11 JER

The study of the origins of words can often be fascinating, particularly in the case of the word "encourage." The prefix *en*
means "to put into" or "to give." The Latin word *cor* means
"heart." The Old French word *corage* is what we call courage.
So when we encourage another person, we put something into
his or her heart. Another way of saying it is that we give
courage to that person. *Merriam-Webster* offers four related
words:

Encourage: suggests the raising of one's confidence especially by an external agency <the teacher's praise *encouraged*
the students to greater efforts>

Inspirit: implies instilling life, energy, courage, or vigor . . .
<patriots *inspirited* the people to resist>

Hearten: implies the lifting of dispiritedness or despon-
dency by an infusion of fresh courage or zeal <a hospital
patient *heartened* by good news>

Embolden: implies the giving of courage sufficient to overcome timidity <*emboldened* by her first success, she tried an
even more difficult climb>

However we look at it, the word "encourage" ranks right up there with the word "affirm" as one of the strongest in our language. Few things are more powerful.

Some of the greatest encouragers we'll ever find are in both books of the Bible. It contains wonderful stories of leaders who brought out the best in people through their own courage and encouragement of those around them. That's why Paul tells us to encourage and strengthen one another.

> *Flatter me, and I may not believe you. Criticize me, and I may not like you. Ignore me, and I may not forgive you. Encourage me, and I may not forget you.*
>
> —WILLIAM ARTHUR WARD

> *Few things in the world are more powerful than a positive push. A smile. A word of optimism and hope. A "you can do it" when things are tough.*
>
> —RICHARD DEVOS

6. Be a source of comfort

> *The tongue that brings healing is a tree of life.*
>
> —PROVERBS 15:4 NIV

> *Blessed are those who mourn, for they will be comforted.*
>
> —MATTHEW 5:4 NIV

Throughout the Scriptures there are countless stories of people suffering. But there is an equal number of stories describing people being comforted. They found their comfort in God and in other people. The Scriptures call upon us to use our own misfortunes and sufferings to help others who are going through something similar.

Although I'm not a biblical scholar, it's probably safe to say that no one in the Old Testament suffered more than Job did. Everything that could go wrong in his life did. One of the more interesting parts of the story is when his three best friends came to comfort him. They tried to explain to him *why* all these bad things were happening. They speculated about his sins and why God was punishing him. But that was no comfort, and it frustrated Job even more. He said to them, "What miserable comforters all of you are" (Job 16:2 TLB). Then he told them that if the situation were reversed, he would treat them differently: "I would speak in such a way that it would help you. I would try to take away your grief" (Job 16:5 TLB). Job has good advice for us. He tells us not to try to figure out or explain the cause of the suffering but to do everything we can to alleviate it.

In the New Testament, Paul wrote eloquently to his friends in Corinth about how we can use our own suffering to help others. He reminded his fellow Christians that Jesus suffered a death almost beyond description. He said that the more we share in that suffering, the more able we are to help others. "This means that if we experience trouble we can pass on to you comfort and spiritual help; for if we ourselves have been comforted we know how to encourage you to endure patiently the same sort of troubles that we ourselves have endured" (2 Corinthians 1:6 PHI).

Because life isn't fair, and because bad things happen to

good people, there are times in all our lives when we need comfort. That comfort usually comes from another person. It can come from the mere presence of a person, from a hug, from holding another's hand, or from kind and reassuring words.

The words of the wise soothe and heal.

—PROVERBS 12:18 TLB

7. Celebrate life!

A cheerful look brings joy to the heart, and good news gives health to the bones.

—PROVERBS 15:30 NIV

I have told you this so that you can share my joy, and that your happiness may be complete.

—JOHN 15:11 PHI

In the previous chapter, I pointed out that the words "joy" and "rejoice" appear in the Scriptures 268 times. That's pretty convincing evidence that God doesn't want us to be sourpusses who walk around complaining that the world and most of the people in it are doomed. God wants us to be joyful and to share our joy with others. He wants us to lighten people's loads and to lift their spirits. We bring out the best in others when we help them become what Zig Ziglar calls "Good Finders." Look for the good, find it, treasure it, talk about it, celebrate it!

In the passages above, Solomon tells us that good news promotes health, and Jesus tells us that our joy should be shared. Yet we live in a society that seems to dwell on bad news, in which people complain and grumble more than they express joy. Maybe this is why Jesus also said, "Let your light shine" (Matthew 5:16 PHI) and Paul tells us that even though we live in a "warped and diseased world" we should be "shining there like lights in a dark place" (Philippians 2:15 PHI).

Early in my teaching career I was struck by all the complaining I heard around campus and in the classroom. Teachers complained about the kids and the administration, and the kids complained about the teachers. Complain, complain, complain. As mentioned in chapter 3, that kind of talk tends to spread and poison the atmosphere. With the help of my students, we improved it, at least in my classroom. I placed a large sign above the chalkboard that read CELEBRATE TODAY! I pointed to it at the beginning of every class and asked, "What are we celebrating today?" They had four options in answering the question: (1) share good news; (2) express thanks for something or someone; (3) say something kind and affirming about a person in the class; (4) make us laugh. As simple as this was, those first few minutes of every class were magical.

Solomon was right. A cheerful heart really is good medicine, and good news really does promote health.

> *When a man is gloomy, everything seems to go wrong;*
> *when he's cheerful, everything seems right!*
>
> *Pleasant sights and good reports give happiness and health.*
> —PROVERBS 15:15, 30 TLB

COMMANDMENT 8

HAVE IMPECCABLE INTEGRITY

IT BRINGS PEACE OF MIND AND A REPUTATION OF HONOR

Old Testament Proverb

The man of integrity walks securely.

—PROVERBS 10:9 NIV

New Testament

Our great desire is to lead a life that is completely honest.

—HEBREWS 13:18 PHI

COMMANDMENT 8

HAVE IMPECCABLE INTEGRITY

IT BRINGS PEACE OF MIND AND A REPUTATION OF HONOR

You deserve honesty from the heart; yes, utter sincerity and truthfulness. Oh give me this wisdom.

—PSALM 51:6 TLB

Blessed are the pure in heart: they shall see God.

—MATTHEW 5:8 JER

WHAT WOULD THE WORLD BE LIKE?

In the Old Testament, Moses, David, Solomon, Job, and Isaiah tell us that the world would be a better place if people honored God's command to be honest in all things and to live lives of integrity. Two of the 10 Commandments tell us to not steal and to not lie. In the New Testament both Jesus and Paul tell us repeatedly to be honest and to be persons of integrity. The author of the letter to the Jewish Christians writes, "We are sure that we have a clear conscience and desire to live honorably in every way" (Hebrews 13:18 NIV). Think for a moment what the world would be like if all the people in it honored these teachings, if every person were honest all the time:

- **Government:** The people who run for office and the ones who hold positions of power would always tell the truth. They would concentrate on working together to make our country better instead of spending so much time and energy making the other party look bad. They would always make decisions with their conscience and without the influence of lobbyists and special interests.

- **Business:** All functions—manufacturing, advertising, sales, investing, and bookkeeping—would be conducted in complete honesty. There would be no rip-offs, no scams, no inflated earnings figures, and no lost pensions.

- **International relations:** Leaders of the world community would be open and forthright with one another. They would cooperate in an honorable manner to negotiate win-win resolutions whenever possible to improve the quality of life around the globe.

- **Personal relationships:** All marriages, friendships, social organizations, and professional networks would be built on a foundation of trust. All the people in them would consistently and fully live up to the commitments they make.

- **Income taxes:** Both individuals and businesses would pay their fair share according to the laws of our country. There would be no illicit schemes, no money laundering, and no cheating of any kind. The government would be in a sound financial position, and taxes would probably be lowered.

- **Sports:** All athletes would be competing on an even playing field. Skill and hard work would be rewarded. There would be no recruiting scandals and no performance-enhancing drugs. All athletic competition would be conducted with integrity.

- **Schools and universities:** There would be academic integrity across the board. Researchers would be scrupulous, teachers would maintain the highest professional standards, and students would earn their credits and grades honestly.

- **Personal security:** The money and possessions we've all earned through hard work and sacrifice would remain safe and secure. We'd honor the Seventh Commandment and respect the ownership rights of all people.

The world would obviously be a much better place if everyone conducted their lives with honesty and integrity. You're probably thinking, "Yes, it would be, but that's a pipe dream and it's never going to happen." You might even be thinking that this author is unduly influenced by his sister—the one named Pollyanna. Not really. I'm simply asking the people who read this to imagine how different the world would be if everyone honored the teachings about honesty and integrity contained in the Scriptures. History tells us that too many people have *not* honored them. And the result is obvious—a world full of crime, theft, cheating, and mistrust. We reap what we sow.

The question isn't whether we can turn everyone into an impeccably honest person and make a perfect world. The question is whether we can make the world a better place by bringing about a higher degree of integrity in our homes, schools, places of business, and governments. It *can* be done. Mother Teresa said we bring about change one person at a time, and Margaret Mead said that it takes only "a few caring people" to start the ball rolling toward significant and positive change on a large scale.

Parents and educators can increase their efforts to both model and teach the value of honesty to our children. All businesses, whether local or international, can establish policies that adhere to the highest ethical standards. And governments at all levels can exercise their power to rewrite the rules and standards of conduct among public officials. All of these things can happen if strong desire is matched with firm commitments. An increase in honesty and integrity wouldn't make the world a perfect place, but it sure would make it a better place.

> *Not only do honest people have stronger, better relationships with others, but their honesty makes them better people and it makes our world a better place.*
> —DR. MIKE THOMSON

THE MEANING OF HONESTY AND INTEGRITY

Integrity is telling myself the truth. And honesty is telling the truth to other people.

—SPENCER JOHNSON

The terms "honesty" and "integrity" are closely related, and are often used as if they're synonymous. But there are some subtle and important differences. Because both are so essential to our quest for fulfillment, it's important to understand both terms fully, including their roots.

Honesty is the first chapter in the book of wisdom.

—THOMAS JEFFERSON

The word "honest" comes from the Latin word *honestus,* which means "honorable," and the French word *honos,* which means "honor." An honorable person is guided by strong moral and ethical principles and consistently attempts to do the right thing. This always results in a clear conscience and wins the respect of others. *Merriam-Webster* defines "honest" as "free from fraud or deception: legitimate, truthful." Additional words used to define it are "genuine," "real," "reputable," "creditable," and "upright."

Integrity means you do what you do because it is right and not just fashionable or politically correct.

—DENIS WAITLEY

The word "integrity" comes from the same Latin root as "integer," which means completeness or wholeness. Similar words are "integral," meaning the core, and "integrated," which means bringing all the parts together. In other words, a person of integrity is one who is not divided—a complete person—one who does not change to fit circumstances. A person of integrity has the same high standards of ethical conduct whether in public or in private. *Merriam-Webster* defines integrity as "firm adherence to a code of especially moral or artistic values: incorruptibility; trustworthiness." It also defines it as "the quality or state of being complete or undivided: completeness."

It's with good reason that the Scriptures tell us to be honest and to live with integrity, and the dictionary helps us understand more fully what the consequences are. Using the words contained in the above definitions, we see the type of person we become when we choose between dishonesty and honesty.

Dishonest people are:	Honest people are:
Fake, phony	Real, genuine
Liars	Truthful
Untrustworthy	Trusted
Dishonored	Honorable
Unethical	Ethical
Corrupt	Incorruptible
Fragmented, divided	Complete, whole
Weak	Strong
Disreputable	Respected

Why Honesty and Integrity Are Crucial

The content of your character is your choice. Day by day, what you do is who you become. Your integrity is your destiny—it is the light that guides your way.

—Heraclitus

Heraclitus was an ancient (sixth century B.C.) Greek philosopher. He came before Socrates and Plato, and, although not as well known, he had a great influence on both of them. He was the first Western philosopher to write extensively about morality, and, as seen in the quotation above, he had strong beliefs about the role integrity plays in determining our ultimate destiny—where and how we end up.

I share Heraclitus's beliefs, because along with humility, integrity is the bedrock of all other virtues. From a spiritual perspective, integrity is an absolute essential. Without it, we'll always be less than what God wants and asks us to be. We can't claim to love God and do dishonest things. Because when we do, we not only disobey the Scriptures, we dishonor our Creator. Lack of integrity is equally costly to nonbelievers. Regardless of our convictions, without integrity we'll always fall short of fulfilling our potential to become fully human, to become the best we can possibly be. Without integrity we'll always be incomplete.

If you're familiar with any of my three previous books, you know that my passion is good character—and the virtues upon which it's built. There's a good reason why integrity and honesty fire up this passion of mine more than any other virtues.

Although I've been "clean" for more than twenty-six years, there was a time in my life when integrity wasn't even on the radar screen. Shortly after enduring the indescribable anguish of my divorce at age twenty-nine, I abandoned God, the teachings of my faith, and most of the cherished values I'd been brought up with. I had a moral meltdown. And I worshiped at the altar of Me for the next ten years.

In looking back on this self-centered, immoral time in my life, I shudder with embarrassment, shame, and remorse. But fortunately, God forgives and offers second chances. He also gives us the opportunity to use our sins and our pain both to grow and to teach others. Part of my writing is cathartic; it helps me exorcise the demons of my past. But more important, it allows me to teach about the direct connection between good character and joyful living.

Those ten years of self-worship and immoral living were fun at first but eventually resulted in a lot of pain. I had never felt so lonely and empty. It was the worst time in my life. My quest to become self-actualized and to raise my self-esteem had instead led to self-loathing. A friend and colleague, who later became a spiritual mentor, led me back to God when I was thirty-nine. It was then that I first became aware of the awesome wisdom contained in the Scriptures. The quality of my life improved dramatically, more than I would have thought possible. Saint Paul's letters to Timothy played a role in that shift.

> *All Scripture is inspired by God and is useful for teaching*
> *the faith and correcting error, for resetting the direction of*
> *a man's life and training him in good living.*
>
> —2 TIMOTHY 3:16 PHI

One of the things that jumped out at me from the pages of the Scriptures was the need to be honest. It made me realize that I'd allowed myself to get sucked into an everyone-does-it mentality. A little dishonesty here and there seemed like no big deal, whether I was looking for tax deductions or trying to maintain relationships with more than one woman at a time. I wasn't an embezzler, a thief, or a compulsive liar, but I wasn't honest all the time either. Several passages in the Scriptures indicted me in that regard, and I made one of the most important choices of my life: I made a commitment to God and to myself that I would never again say or do anything dishonest.

There are no words in our language that come close to describing the rewards of that decision. The Scriptures did, indeed, help me correct my errors and reset the direction of my life. They did, indeed, train me in the good living that Paul wrote about. Life offers few things better than peace of mind.

There is no pillow so soft as a clear conscience.
—French proverb

The everyone-does-it mentality of the 1970s still flourishes today. Add to it the belief that "it's wrong only if you get caught," and we have a deadly mixture. There are all kinds of ways to rationalize dishonesty. It starts with our government. Very few citizens believe that the people who run our country are honest. We repeatedly read about the influence of lobbyists, outright bribes, and other forms of scandal. Some people argue that if the people running our government can cheat, we should be able to do the same. There are two flaws in this line of thinking. The first is that only a small percentage of people in our government cheat. They get far more publicity than the ones with integrity. I'd like to believe that the overwhelming majority of our government leaders are honest public servants. Our system would collapse if they weren't. The second problem is that the "everybody's doing it" mentality only compounds the problem. No matter who's doing it, there's no justification for being dishonest.

CAN INTEGRITY BE TAUGHT? THREE STRATEGIES FOR PLANTING SOME SEEDS

I believe it's due to this deeply imbedded mind-set that everyone is dishonest—from people in the highest levels of government to the next-door neighbor—that integrity was the most difficult concept I ever taught. Whether I was teaching psychology to high school seniors or organizational behavior to adults at the university, my lessons on honesty and integrity were met with great resistance. The notion that everyone does dishonest things and that you have to be dishonest if you want to compete in the world is a tough one to overcome, but I do think I made some progress. Many students thanked me for teaching them about the real meaning of success and the part that integrity plays in it. They also claimed that it was making a real difference in their lives. Others were reluctant to go that far, but at least I'd planted some seeds.

Over the years, through a lot of trial and error, I developed three strategies that seemed to work with most of my students.

Ten Questions

My first strategy was a handout—a sheet of paper posing the following ten questions. I asked the students to answer each of them "Yes" or "No," in writing:

1. If you bought any product, from a car to a blender, would you want the salesperson to be honest with you?

2. If you owned a business, would you want your employees to be honest in dealing with customers and in submitting expense accounts?

3. If you were riding in a cab, would you want the driver to take the most direct route and charge you fairly?

4. If you lost your wallet, along with cash, driver's license, and credit cards, would you want the person who found it to return it to you intact?

5. If you invested some of your hard-earned money, would you want the financial adviser to be completely up-front with you?

6. If you're married or in a serious relationship, do you want your loved one to be honest with you?

7. If you were competing in an athletic event, would you want the officials and your opponents to conduct themselves honorably?

8. If you're an employee, do you want your work and achievements to be evaluated fairly, honestly, and on their merits?

9. If you bought a product with your credit card over the phone or the Internet, would you want the person handling the transaction to honor your privacy and security?

10. If you were a recording artist or studio owner, would you want people to buy your music in a legal and honest manner?

In all the years I asked these questions, no one ever gave a "No" answer—not one!—in response to any of them. So we all agreed, and these questions led to some great discussions about honesty, integrity, and the Golden Rule. One year a high school senior offered an interesting—and revealing—response to these ten questions. He read them, answered all of them "Yes," and then commented out loud, "Yeah, but this is different." I knew what he meant but asked him to explain. He said, "No one wants to be ripped off. No one wants to be cheated. These questions are all about what other people do to us." I asked him, "How is that different from what you do to other people?" His response was "Oh, I see what you're getting at." Hopefully, I scored a point—or at least got him to think.

FOUR CHOICES

The other activity that seemed to make inroads regarding the importance of honesty and integrity had to do with life choices. I gave all the students a small piece of paper and asked them to write down the four most important choices (aside from faith) that they thought they'd ever make in their lifetimes. No one was to talk until everyone had written down his or her four choices. Not surprisingly, the four choices that came up most often were:

1. Education
2. Career
3. Marriage
4. Where to live

I told my students I agreed that these were all important choices. But I wanted to point out some other choices they might have overlooked, possibly because they'd never considered them to be choices. Here are the four I gave them:

1. Attitude
2. Respect/kindness
3. Work ethic
4. Honesty/integrity

I've written about all of these topics in previous books, so I won't elaborate on them here. But I do want to summarize my teachings on them and make a special point about the fourth one.

- **Attitude:** It's the engine that runs everything. The most important thing to understand about it is that it will always be a choice, no matter what circumstances we find ourselves in. See chapter 5 in *Life's Greatest Lessons:* "Attitude Is a Choice—the Most Important One You'll Ever Make."

- **Respect/kindness:** The Golden Rule says we should treat other people as we'd like to be treated by them. It doesn't say to treat them well only when they're being nice, and it doesn't say to treat them well only when we're in a good mood. How we treat others, regardless of circumstances, is always a choice. See chapters 8 and 10 in *Life's Greatest Lessons:* "Good People Build Their Lives on a Foundation of Respect" and "Kind Words Cost Little, but Accomplish Much."

- **Work ethic:** How hard we work determines how far we'll go. It's a choice we make whether we're in school, in a relationship, in our career, or in an athletic competition. And it's a choice we make every day of our lives. See chapter 13 in *Life's Greatest Lessons:* "There's No Substitute for Hard Work."

- **Honesty/integrity:** I also wrote about this topic in *Life's Greatest Lessons.* Chapter 9 is "Honesty Is Still the Best Policy." I've chosen to write about it again in this book for two reasons: first, because it's a topic important enough to re-examine; and second, because it wasn't discussed from a biblical perspective in my first book.

Virtually everyone will agree with me that a person will go far in life if he or she consistently does three things: keeps a positive attitude, treats other people with respect and kindness, and works to the best of his or her ability. The percentage of people who maintain these high standards on a regular basis is small. But those who do all have something in common: they succeed in life. It's a great formula for success, but it isn't enough. It isn't complete until we add honesty and integrity.

As I write this book, the final pieces of the horrendous Enron scandal are playing out. Leading up to it were the scandals involving Tyco, Arthur Andersen, Xerox, WorldCom, Merrill Lynch, and a number of others. Back in the early eighties it was Ivan Boesky and Michael Milken. Before them it was, well, someone else. And I'm keeping government scandals out of it. The people who were brought down in all of these tragedies had some things in common: they had a positive attitude—a strong desire to succeed; they treated their business associates (the ones they were making deals with) diplomatically and respectfully; and they put in long hours of hard work. And they all proved my point: attitude, respect, and hard work aren't enough. They ruined their own lives and damaged the lives of countless others because they were missing an essential ingredient: integrity. We reap what we sow.

CONSEQUENCES AND REWARDS

A good man is guided by his honesty; the evil man is destroyed by his dishonesty.

—PROVERBS 11:3 TLB

This third approach was one I conducted in small groups. Each group of four to five students was given a sheet of paper with two columns at the top. The one on the left was headed "Consequences of dishonesty," while the one on the right was "Rewards of integrity." I asked my students to brainstorm with one another, then list as many things under each heading that they could come up with. Both my high school students and the adults at the university became very engaged, and the discussions within the small groups were lively. Below are the consequences and rewards we came up with over a period of almost twenty years. I wrote about some of them in my first book, but ever the teacher who likes to reinforce his points, I think they're well worth including here along with a few new ones.

THE CONSEQUENCES OF DISHONESTY

Lies will get any man into trouble.

—PROVERBS 12:13 TLB

He who takes crooked paths will be found out.

—PROVERBS 10:9 NIV

Here's the list my students and I developed:

- **Dishonesty ruins relationships.** Consider the relationships among people in the following social institutions: marriage, friendship, business, school, sports, place of worship, and government. If those relationships are strong, it's because of the solid foundation they're built upon—trust. When someone violates that trust, the foundation is gone and the relationship crumbles.

- **Dishonesty damages reputations.** People who lie and do other dishonest things are quickly discovered and just as quickly develop a bad reputation. They lose their credibility, and others stop believing them even when they're telling the truth. After a person does something dishonest, he puts a question mark after all his future acts. The simple truth is that no one wants to deal with a dishonest person.

- **Dishonesty ends careers.** The desire to get ahead in one's career is so strong among many people, they're willing to sacrifice their integrity in pursuit of that next step up the corporate ladder. Examples include lying on a résumé and taking credit for someone else's achievements. And because they eventually get caught, they end up being fired or demoted, ruining any chance to attain their dream.

- **Dishonesty becomes a habit.** When a person does something dishonest and gets away with it, the temptation to do it again becomes almost irresistible. A good example is a student who copies someone else's homework instead of doing it himself. As with most acts of dishonesty, cheating becomes an easier way to get things done—a moral shortcut. Then it's a habit, a morally lazy way of life.

- **Dishonesty often leads to punishment.** The penalties for those caught being dishonest can be severe. There are thousands of people in jails and prisons throughout the country who can attest to that. Even those who don't get into trouble with the law can suffer enormously. What's worse than losing a friend, your career, or your reputation?

- **Dishonesty hurts innocent people.** The dishonest person isn't the only one who suffers. Being betrayed is a terrible, sometimes life-changing experience. Few things hurt more or are more unfair. The saddest part is that the people who feel the pain are completely innocent. And that's not all. When a loved one is exposed for doing something dishonest, it often brings shame and embarrassment to families, friends, even entire communities.

- **Dishonesty damages health.** Few people realize that dishonesty can trigger both physical and psychological problems. Dr. Lewis Andrews, a psychologist who's studied the effects of dishonesty on the central nervous system for many years, says that every act of deceit has a negative consequence on our health. It causes stress and strain. People who do dishonest things literally attack their own well-being.

- **Dishonesty divides us.** This is one of the worst consequences of dishonesty. A dishonest life is a divided life, one that holds no hope of attaining its potential—to become a complete human being. Those who lie and cheat will never know the satisfaction and joy of being the authentic person God calls us to be throughout the Scriptures.

The Rewards of Integrity

In my integrity you uphold me and set me in your presence forever.

—Psalm 41:12 NIV

Anyone whose ways are honourable walks secure.

—Proverbs 10:9 JER

On a more positive note, we also came up with this list:

- **Integrity brings peace of mind.** A clear conscience is something every man and woman of integrity enjoys. They don't ever have to worry about getting caught; they don't ever need to explain themselves out of a jam. Integrity has many rewards. Among them are peace of mind, a good night's sleep, confidence, and self-esteem.

- **Integrity builds good character.** A person of integrity and a person of good character are virtually the same. There can't be one without the other. While a person of good character has many other positive traits, the cornerstones are humility and integrity. Not only do they lead to admirable qualities, they lead to respect and a solid reputation.

- **Integrity cements relationships.** Trust, the foundation of all good relationships, is dependent upon integrity. Every kind of relationship flourishes when the people involved know they can count on each other. Integrity is the glue that holds these relationships together, particularly during challenging times.

- **Integrity makes people complete.** The great psychologist Carl Jung said that our deepest desire is for a feeling of "wholeness." In other words, we want to become the type of person that we're capable of being. Integrity is the quality that makes this possible. Without it, we feel as though something is missing. That void is filled with integrity, which literally means to be complete.

- **Integrity promotes good health.** People with impeccable integrity enjoy mental health at the deepest level. Their minds are at ease because they've freed themselves of guilt, worry, and other forms of inner turmoil. They have less stress and are less prone to illness. Doing the right thing on a consistent basis makes you feel healthy and vibrant.

- **Integrity helps us become authentic.** William Shakespeare advised us hundreds of years ago, "This above all, to thine own self be true." Only a few years ago Spencer Johnson said, "Integrity is telling myself the truth." Integrity is an inside job. It begins by being real, genuine, authentic, sincere. When we're true to ourselves, we'll be true to others too.

There are good reasons why integrity and honesty are discussed so often in both the Old and New Testaments. The authors had a profound understanding of human nature. They knew our weaknesses and the temptations we would face—and they wrote the Scriptures to help us deal with those very challenges. They can help us make good choices, develop good character, and fulfill God's plan for us.

> *I know, my God, that you test the heart and are pleased with integrity.*
> —1 Chronicles 29:17 NIV

> *The time is always right to do what is right.*
> —Martin Luther King, Jr.

HELP THOSE IN NEED

IT REALLY IS BETTER TO GIVE THAN TO RECEIVE

Old Testament Proverb

One man gives freely, yet gains even more . . .
A generous man will prosper; he who refreshes others will
himself be refreshed.

—PROVERBS 11:24–25 NIV

New Testament

For if you give, you will get! Your gift will return to you
in full and overflowing measure, pressed down, shaken
together to make room for more, and running over.
Whatever measure you use to give—large or small—will
be used to measure what is given back to you.

—LUKE 6:38 TLB

Commandment 9

Help those in need
It really is better to give than to receive

You'll not likely go wrong here if you keep remembering that our Master said, "You're far happier giving than getting."

—Acts 20:35 MES

Life's Greatest Paradox

Life is full of paradoxes, or apparent contradictions that somehow ring true. Here are four that we hear often:

"Less is more."
"Opposites attract."
"They have a love-hate relationship."
"Our greatest strength can be our greatest weakness."

But the biggest paradox of all is . . .

"The More We Give, the More We Get."

How can this be true? The messages the media bombards us with urge us in a completely different direction: get, buy, obtain, earn, win, gain, acquire, increase, add. They're the mantras of capitalism, as summed up on the familiar bumper stickers: "He who dies with the most toys wins" and "Life is a game, and money is the way we keep score." While I'm all for the freedoms we enjoy living in a democratic nation and a capitalistic society, I'm also keenly aware that all good things have their dark side—yet another paradox. As I wrote back in the first two chapters, it's easy to be seduced by popular culture, and it's easy to fall in love with money and possessions. We're hounded daily by messages that tell us: Less isn't more—more is more! Get more!

When I asked my high school and adult students to respond to the statement "It's better to give than to receive," the answers I got were no surprise. I gave each student a slip of paper, told them I was going to make a brief statement, and asked them to write down the first thought that popped into their heads. These were the most common responses:

"Yeah, right."
"No way!"
"Sounds like something from the Bible."
"False."
"Bull——"
"Wrong."

"Written by a liberal, no doubt."
"That's what they tell you in church."
"No, it's the opposite."
"Not in the real world."
"Only lazy people believe that crap."

There were a few who agreed with the message, but the overwhelming majority was frankly opposed. During the discussion that followed, a few courageous students spoke up, affirming the truth of those words. Most people, they said, don't understand the joy of giving because they've never tried it. I describe these students as courageous because they ran the risk of being labeled Communists, socialists, bleeding-heart liberals, or all three. And those terms did come up almost every time I did this exercise. But the discussions that followed were always of value, provided I could serve as an effective referee and help the "getters" keep their emotions in check.

Throughout my teaching career I often wrote the words of well-known and respected people on the board to start or enhance a discussion. In this case, I used two:

> *The value of a man resides in what he gives and not in what he is capable of receiving.*
>
> —ALBERT EINSTEIN

> *I have found that among its other benefits, giving liberates the soul of the giver.*
>
> —MAYA ANGELOU

In the previous chapter I pointed out that we can't be complete human beings if we choose to live lives lacking integrity. The word itself means wholeness. And an important aspect of being a complete person is becoming sensitive to the needs of others and doing what we can to help them when we can. As Albert Einstein and Maya Angelou point out, we give not because we have to but because we need to. It enhances the lives of others, it builds stronger communities, and it revitalizes the spirit of the giver.

Our discussions in class about getting and giving didn't always shift the majority to the givers' side, but they did plant some seeds. Even the students who described themselves as "hard-core capitalists" admitted that giving can result in enormous benefits. One of them is a better society. Individuals and foundations achieve incredible things in this country every year because thousands of generous people feel a moral and/or spiritual obligation to give back for the good of all.

Thousands of years ago, leading figures in the Bible had a clear understanding of this great paradox. Solomon wrote that one who gives freely gains even more (Proverbs 11:24 NIV). Jesus used almost the same words: "Your gift will return to you in full and overflowing measure" (Luke 6:38 TLB). Many people are reluctant to give at first but increase their giving as soon as they realize the far-reaching rewards for both the receiver and the giver.

I had a dear friend and colleague who was deeply religious. He knew the Bible as well as anyone I'd ever known, and he applied its teachings to every aspect of his life. He was also loved and respected by everyone on staff. One day he told me something about giving that I found hard to believe, even though I knew him to be scrupulously honest. I'd just told him that I wasn't really able to give much to worthy causes because of my meager teacher's salary and the enormous appetites and alarming growth rates of my three boys. He smiled knowingly and said, "The more you give, the more you'll receive." To which I replied, "But not if you don't have anything to give."

He said that he too had once found it hard to take that when we give we get even more back. He was a teacher too, after all, and had not much more to give than I had. But he took a leap of faith and was astounded at the result. He gave more than he thought he could, wanting to put this biblical teaching to the test. A short time later he was blessed with an unexpected windfall. He said it seemed "freaky" at first, like a miracle, but then realized it was simply biblical truth in action. And he soon came to realize that the more he gave, the more he received, which included the sheer joy of contributing to an important cause.

Since that time many years ago I've heard countless stories like his about the miracle of giving and the give/receive principle explained by Solomon and Jesus. I've also experienced it personally every time I give. I'm not suggesting we look at giving as investing—that we should expect a good return on our money—but I *am* suggesting that we give and trust God to be true to his word. We give because we want to give, because we can help someone, and because it's always a win-win proposition.

A year before this writing I made a bigger-than-usual contribution to a special drive we were having at my church. It was a little beyond my comfort zone, but I was confident that it was the right thing to do. A few days later the deacon called to ask if he could come and see me in my home. I figured he was coming over to thank me for my donation and thought he was making a nice gesture. He did thank me, but also asked me to increase my donation by 150 percent. He said, "We figured that if you could afford to give what you did, you can probably afford to give more." As soon as he said this, I realized that he was right. I had done more speaking than usual that month, and enough money would be coming in to cover the increased donation and still leave me with a little extra. "One man gives freely, yet gains even more" (Proverbs 11:24 NIV).

A year later I saw another glaring need at our church. I offered to pay for it, thinking it would add up to the same amount I had given the previous year. But the job turned out to be much bigger and more complicated than it looked, and I was informed that it would be four times what I'd expected. My first thought was "Why did I have to open my big mouth?" My second one was "Now how am I going to get out of this?" I talked to my wife, Cathy, about it, figuring she'd have the answer, but our conversation soon turned to how richly we'd been blessed in the past year. We made the donation. A few weeks later my semiannual royalty check arrived. For the past three years each one had been for about the same modest amount. This one was four times the usual. "Your gift will return to you in full and in overflowing measure" (Luke 6:38 TLB).

I share these stories with you not to make myself look like a hero but to prove a point about biblical truth and wisdom: It really is better to give than to receive. We reap what we sow.

It is one of the most beautiful compensations of this life that no man can sincerely try to help another without helping himself.

—RALPH WALDO EMERSON

TWO KINDS OF NEEDS, TWO KINDS OF HELP

When you saw the title of this chapter ("Help Those in Need"), what did you think? Did it make you think of the desperately poor? Those lacking the most basic necessities? For sure, that's *one* kind of need. The severity of poverty both in this country and around the world is staggering. But there are many other types of need. For every person in need of financial help, there's another in need of a different kind of help. The Scriptures address them all.

HELPING PEOPLE WHO ARE POOR

He who gives to the poor will lack nothing.

—PROVERBS 28:27 NIV

According to the U.S. Census Bureau, almost 36 million people in this country live in poverty. That's more than 12 percent of our total population. And as we know, the rate is far higher in many other countries, as more than 30 percent of the world's population lives in poverty. It's not my purpose here to examine *why* there's so much poverty, to pin the blame on anyone, or to offer a quick fix for the problem. But I do want to remind my readers that all they have to do is take a good look around to see people going hungry and without the basic necessities. It's also my purpose to point out that helping the poor, the needy, and the oppressed is a major theme in the Scriptures. To be more precise, it's mentioned 94 times in the Old Testament and 20 times in the New Testament. Those many passages might best be summarized with these two:

> *There will always be poor people in the land. Therefore I command you to be openhanded toward your brothers and toward the poor and needy in your land.*
>
> —DEUTERONOMY 15:11 NIV

> *If you see some brother or sister in need and have the means to do something about it but turn a cold shoulder and do nothing, what happens to God's love? It disappears. And you made it disappear.*
>
> —JOHN 3:17 MES

The Scriptures don't tell us that we're bad because we enjoy a comfortable life or that we should feel guilty if we've worked hard and earned good lives for ourselves and our families. Many of God's leaders in both the Old and New Testaments had both money and earthly possessions. It's not *having* them that makes us bad; it's not *sharing* them with the less fortunate that makes us bad. The Scriptures don't tell us to solve the problems of all the poor; they tell us to help the poor around us and that we'll be blessed ourselves when we do.

There's no shortage of opportunities to do this. Here are a few simple examples:

- Donate money and/or possessions to a charitable organization.
- Buy a poor person a meal.
- Donate money on a regular basis to a group that helps the poor.
- Give a generous tip to someone who's among the working poor.
- Donate some of your time to a charitable organization.
- Buy something special for a family in need.

Giving to the poor is always a win-win-win situation. It helps others, it makes us more complete, and it honors God.

He who refreshes others will himself be refreshed.

—PROVERBS 11:25 NIV

Your gift will return to you in full and overflowing measure.

—LUKE 6:38 TLB

HELPING PEOPLE WHO ARE IN NEED

Carry each other's burdens.
Let us not grow tired of doing good.
Let us then do good to all men as opportunity offers.

—GALATIANS 6:2, 9, 10 PHI

We're all in need of help. Life would be literally impossible to navigate without the help of others. Conversely, we regularly come into contact with people who need our help. Even the great psalmist King David admitted to God that he was "needy." He was keenly aware of his own weaknesses, and he asked God to be his "rock of refuge" (Psalms 70:5 and 71:3 NIV). There are people in need all around us on an almost daily basis. They have physical, emotional, social, and spiritual needs, and if we pay more attention and give a little more of ourselves, we can lighten their burdens.

Throughout the Scriptures we're told to help not only poor people but people with the following hardships:

ILLNESS
I was ill and you came and looked after me.

—MATTHEW 25:36 PHI

I don't know anyone who's healthy *all* the time. We all get sick. When it happens, the thing we want most is to get better, but until we do, we could use a little attention and kindness from others. Because each of us encounters so many sick people throughout our lives, we have countless opportunities to do good. We can send them cards and letters, visit them, run errands for them, call them, and let them know they're in our thoughts and prayers. These little gestures can have a powerful impact.

DISABILITY
Soon some men arrived carrying a paralytic on a small
bed. . . . When they failed to find a way of getting him in

because of the dense crowd, they went up to the top of the house and let him down, bed and all.

—LUKE 5:18–19 PHI

We're rarely called upon to do something as dramatic as lowering a paralyzed man through a hole in a roof, but the Scriptures do tell us to help the crippled, the blind, the lame, and the afflicted. Whether limited because of a physical or mental handicap, these people need assistance in many of the daily tasks we do for ourselves without even thinking. We should never miss an opportunity to help those who are in daily need of a helping hand.

LONELINESS
I was lonely and you made me welcome.

—MATTHEW 25:36 PHI

For a lot of different reasons, people of all ages suffer from the feeling that they're disconnected from the rest of the world. An elderly person in a retirement home or a sensitive child who feels lost in a large school can feel equally isolated. We can alleviate some of their pain by simply reaching out to them, by showing an interest. Our strongest psychological need is to feel that there's some significance in our lives. Lonely people feel as though they don't count, and we can often bring much joy to their lives just by showing them that they do.

EMOTIONAL PAIN

For he gives us comfort in our trials so that we in turn may be able to give the same sort of strong sympathy to others in theirs.

—2 CORINTHIANS 1:4 PHI

It's pretty hard to escape having you psyche dinged up from time to time. That's just life. People do hurt each other physically, but more often they hurt each other emotionally, sometimes even cripple each other. Just as serious physical wounds need treatment, so do emotional wounds. The Scriptures tell that we should "comfort those in any trouble" (2 Corinthians 1:4 NIV). We've all experienced a variety of emotional wounds. And most of those wounds were healed by the comforting words of people who cared. We can do the same thing for others.

DISCOURAGEMENT

Therefore encourage one another and build each other up.

—1 THESSALONIANS 5:11 NIV

Because life is hard and not always fair, we all experience quite a few disappointments along the way. It's natural to become discouraged—literally to lose our courage. Maybe that's why the word "encourage" and other forms of it appear more than 60 times in the Scriptures. Everyone gets down from time to time and needs a few words of encouragement. When we encourage others, we give them courage. There's no greater gift. It can be life-changing.

There's really no such thing as a "self-made" man or woman. Every successful person who ever lived has benefited from the help and encouragement of other people—parents, spouses, friends, teachers, coaches, pastors, colleagues, sometimes even strangers. There are few things more powerful and few things more effective than encouragement for bringing out the best in others—and in ourselves.

> *You need to be aware of what others are doing, applaud their efforts, acknowledge their successes, and encourage them in their pursuits. When we all help one another, everybody wins.*
>
> —Jim Stovall

Imprisonment
I was in prison and you came to see me there.
—Matthew 25:36 PHI

Until recent years, I never gave much thought to people in prisons and jails. I figured that they were probably locked up for a good reason. They'd violated our laws and were now paying the price—end of story. That paradigm shifted dramatically when I received my first letter from a person who wrote me from prison. My book *Life's Greatest Lessons* had somehow found its way into the system when I was still a self-published author. A young man with limited skills in English read it and then wrote me a heart-wrenching letter from his cell in Miami. That changed everything.

Since that time I've received additional letters from several other imprisoned men and one woman from around the country. The letters are always long and always just as sad as they are heartwarming. They're sad because these people all got off to a bad start in life, most of them as the victims of abuse. Many of them bounced around from home to foster home to youth detention center, and eventually to jail and prison. Their stories include episodes of physical and verbal abuse, rejection, loneliness, anger, alcohol, drugs, bad associations, and then crime.

The heartwarming part is their sincere effort to resurrect their lives. Many of them have completed high school while incarcerated, have had religious conversions, and have benefited from counseling. They've read extensively about personal growth and have committed themselves to becoming responsible, productive citizens. These letters remind me that the Scriptures contain a central message of hope. The Bible is full of stories about people who committed atrocious crimes, then found grace: people who repented, made amends for their sins, were forgiven, and moved on to live fruitful lives.

I'm not suggesting that the Bible tells us all to join ministries that serve people who've been convicted of crimes. But there are a few things we *can* do. The first is to change our thinking. There's a tendency to think the worst of both prisons and prisoners. Of course we'd all like to see the remorseless perpetrators of the most atrocious crimes locked up. But there are countless other people in jails and prisons who started their lives as victims, made mistakes, have apologized, are now paying their debts, and are sincerely trying to better themselves.

According to the Scriptures, we need to change our hearts about these people and help them when it's feasible. Several faiths have effective prison ministries that provide us with the opportunity to help by praying, contributing financially, helping family members, writing letters, and donating paperback books. Many prisoners deserve our empathy and our compassion.

> *Think constantly of those in prison as if you were prisoners at their side.*
>
> —HEBREWS 13:3 PHI

OPPRESSION

> *If you do away with the yoke of oppression, with the pointing finger and malicious talk, and if you spend yourselves in behalf of the hungry and satisfy the needs of the oppressed, then your light will rise in the darkness, and your night will become like the noonday.*
>
> —ISAIAH 58:9–10 NIV

Merriam-Webster defines oppression as "unjust or cruel exercise of authority or power; a sense of being weighed down in body or mind: depression." Sadly, oppression has existed since the dawn of mankind. It's recorded in history, and it's with us today throughout the world. Our own history is replete with stories of oppression against Native Americans, African Americans, immigrants, minorities, women, members of particular faiths, political dissenters, homosexuals, and the working poor, to mention a few. Certainly, we have far fewer oppressed people in our country today, but the problem remains for many, even if they're not in our backyards.

Sometimes our political views determine who we see as the oppressed and the oppressors, but I think we'd all agree that there are thousands, maybe millions, of people in our country who feel burdened and even crushed. The Scriptures tell us to help those people. We're not told to rid the world or our country of oppression but to do what we can. We can't all be Mahatma Gandhi; Martin Luther King, Jr.; or Mother Teresa; but we *can* lighten the load of the oppressed around us.

"Gifts Differing"—You Can't Do It All

It's not my intention to guilt-trip anyone into leading a more generous life. But it *is* my intention to help raise awareness of the needs around us and to encourage people to be more giving of themselves. It helps others, and it comes back to us in "overflowing measure." The Scriptures don't command us to devote our entire lives to the service of others, but they do tell us to help and serve others regularly. They remind us that we're not all equipped for every type of service but that we should use the gifts we've been given to enhance the lives of people in need.

In the old King James translation of the Bible, Saint Paul tells us that we have "gifts differing according to the grace which has been given to us" (Romans 12:6). In other words, we can't do it all because we're not equipped to do it all. But we can use *our* particular gifts to serve others.

Through the grace of God we have different gifts. Let the man who is called to give, give freely; let the man who wields authority think of his responsibility; and let the man who feels sympathy for his fellows act cheerfully.

—ROMANS 12:6 PHI

GIVE QUIETLY, GIVE CHEERFULLY

Beware of doing your good deeds conspicuously to catch men's eyes or you will miss the reward of your Heavenly Father. So, when you do good to other people, don't hire a trumpeter to go in front of you.

—MATTHEW 6:1–2 PHI

Each man should give what he has decided in his heart to give, not reluctantly or under compulsion, for God loves a cheerful giver.

—2 CORINTHIANS 9:7 NIV

Several years ago a fellow member of the congregation gave a sizable donation to the church I belonged to at the time. Apparently, he didn't take either of the two passages above to heart because ultimately the experience made him angry. He told several people that he was mad for two reasons. First, his gift was a big sacrifice. He could have used it, if he'd traded in his Mercedes, to buy a new model. Second, his gift wasn't openly acknowledged. The pastor didn't thank him publicly at any of the worship services. One of the associate pastors had a talk with the man after learning of his displeasure. He pointed out the teachings of the Scriptures on giving and suggested that maybe the donation had been made in the wrong spirit. That made him even angrier, and he left the church. He said he'd find a new one that would appreciate his generosity.

A few years later a teacher friend of mine who belonged to the same church told me privately that he had inherited a house worth about $400,000. His annual salary at the time was about one tenth of that. I was happy for him. A couple of weeks later I learned at a meeting of the elders that my friend had given the property to the church to help meet the housing needs of an associate pastor. He donated it under the condition that the gift remain anonymous. When I talked to him about it later, he said, "I already have a home, and the church needed another one a lot more than I did. It was the right thing to do. I felt so blessed to be able to do it. I've never done anything more joyful in my life."

Two large gifts: one given in the wrong spirit that resulted in anger and one given in the right spirit that resulted in joy.

SERVICE, PURPOSE, AND JOY

We receive from life what we give, and in the process we understand more of what it means to discover our purpose.
—RICHARD J. LEIDER

This is the true joy in life, the being used for a purpose recognized by yourself as a mighty one.
—GEORGE BERNARD SHAW

I began this chapter explaining one of the great paradoxes of life: the more we give, the more we get. I want to end it by reinforcing this same point. Solomon, Jesus, and many others in the Scriptures not only tell us to give, to serve, and to help others, they also point out that it will come back to us. In fact, more will be returned to us than what we give. That doesn't mean that if we give a thousand dollars, fifteen hundred dollars will come back to us, and it doesn't mean that if we devote ten hours of service to others, someone else will devote fifteen hours of service to us. What it *does* mean is that life will be richer. We'll be less self-centered and materialistic. We'll be more humble and giving. We'll find more purpose, be more fulfilled, and know the true joy of life as we've never known it before.

> *For it is in giving that we receive.*
>
> —SAINT FRANCIS OF ASSISI

COMMANDMENT 10

DO EVERYTHING IN LOVE

IT'S THE ONLY WAY TO FIND TRUE PEACE AND FULFILLMENT

Old Testament Proverb

Let love and faithfulness never leave you; bind them around your neck, write them on the tablet of your heart.

—PROVERBS 3:3 NIV

New Testament

Let everything that you do be done in love.

—1 CORINTHIANS 16:14 PHI

For the original command, as you know, is that we should love one another.

—1 JOHN 3:11 PHI

DO EVERYTHING IN LOVE

IT'S THE ONLY WAY TO FIND TRUE PEACE AND FULFILLMENT

Let us not love merely in theory or in words—let us love in sincerity and in practice.

—1 JOHN 3:18 PHI

LOVE: THE MOST DIFFICULT WORD TO DEFINE AND THE MOST DIFFICULT VIRTUE TO PRACTICE

We often throw words about casually without a lot of thought as to the real meaning of them. That's why whenever I write a book or an article or prepare a speech, the first thing I put on my desk is the dictionary. I want to be as precise as I can so readers have a clear understanding of what I'm trying to say. Since "love" is one of the most used, abused, and misunderstood words in the English language, I knew I was in for a challenge in defining it, even with the help of *Merriam-Webster.* And I knew I was in real trouble when I looked up the word on Wikipedia, the free online encyclopedia. It advised me, "Love is commonly considered impossible to define."

Love has been the subject of countless movies, books, poems, essays, stories, songs, quotations, and legends, but that doesn't really bring us any closer to a definition, as everyone seems to have his or her own. For clarity's sake, though, it's important to define love as I write about it in this book and as it's used in the Scriptures. The dictionary is still a valuable starting place, and the first three definitions in *Merriam-Webster* are helpful: (1) "strong affection for another arising out of kinship or personal ties"; (2) "attraction based on sexual desire: affection and tenderness felt by lovers"; (3) "affection based on admiration, benevolence, or common interests." But further down in this list of several definitions of love is the best one for purposes of this book:

> *Love: Unselfish loyal and benevolent concern for the good of another: as (1): the fatherly concern of God for humankind (2): brotherly concern for others.*

Although there are many types of love—romantic love, love of family, love of friends, and love of country among them—I'm going to zero in here on the types of love discussed in the Bible. While there are more than six hundred references to love in the Scriptures, they can be divided into two simple categories. The first one is the love between God and man, the second is the love we have for each other. Paradoxically (again!), it's impossible to separate them.

> *If you really love me, you will keep the commandments I have given you.*
>
> —JOHN 14:15 PHI

> *This is my commandment: that you love each other as I have loved you.*
>
> —JOHN 15:12 PHI

There are millions of people in this country and other countries who claim to love God. I don't doubt the sincerity of their claim. But saying we love God is the easy part. Keeping his commandments is the hard part, especially the one that tells us to love one another. To make it even more challenging, we're given another related commandment:

> *Let everything that you do be done in love.*
>
> —I CORINTHIANS 16:14 PHI

Back in chapter 4, I wrote that the Bible tells us to not judge others. I also wrote that it's the second most difficult challenge contained in the Scriptures. What tops the list? Although some may disagree, I think doing everything in love is the hardest of all. We're not told to do *some* things in love or to do *most* things in love, but to do *everything* in love. Seemingly impossible? Yes. Actually impossible? No.

LOVE: IT'S NOT ONLY UNSELFISH, IT'S HARD WORK

> *Practice giving love instead of taking love.*
>
> —RYUHO OKAWA

Love is hard work.

—MIGUEL ALGARIN

There are two exceedingly common misperceptions about what love is. The first is that love is something we not only deserve but have a right to expect from others. This belief is based on a universal human flaw (we all have it to some degree): selfishness. We think that love is something we get, not something we give. The second misguided notion is that love is a nice cozy feeling that happens naturally and requires no work on our part. Wrong on both counts—love is in giving, not getting, and it's very hard work.

In order to better explain what genuine love is, I'll rely on two authors who have had a profound influence on my thinking. The first is Erich Fromm (1900–1980), a Jewish psychotherapist from Germany; the second is John Powell, a Catholic priest and retired theologian from Chicago. What Fromm wrote in *The Art of Loving* in 1956 and Powell echoed in *Unconditional Love* in 1978 explains what love is more eloquently and concisely than this author ever could. So rather than paraphrase their writings, I'll let them speak in their own words.

> *In the most general way, the active character of love can be described by stating that love is primarily giving, not receiving. . . .*
>
> *The most widespread misunderstanding is that which assumes that giving is "giving up" something, being deprived of, sacrificing. . . .*
>
> *For the productive character, giving has an entirely different meaning. Giving is more joyous than receiving,*

not because it is a deprivation, but because in the act of giving lies the expression of my aliveness. . . .

In the act of giving something is born, and both persons involved are grateful for the life that is born for both of them. Specifically with regard to love this means: love is a power which produces love.

—ERICH FROMM

True love is unconditional. There is no third possibility: love is either conditional or unconditional. Either I attach conditions to my love for you or I do not. To the extent that I do attach such conditions, I do not really love you. I am only offering an exchange, not a gift. And true love is and must always be a free gift. A meaningful life can result only from the experience of love, and this implies a commitment and a dedication. . . .

Saying "Yes!" to God is not a simple matter because making our lives into lives of love is not a simple or easy thing. . . .

Giving the gift of myself in love leaves me with a deep and lasting satisfaction of having done something good with my life.

—JOHN POWELL, S.J.

What the Scriptures Say About Love

God is love, and anyone who lives in love is living with God and God is living in him.

— 1 John 4:16 TLB

Although I'm not an expert on the Bible, I think most scholars who've studied it extensively would agree with me that love is presented somewhat differently in the Old and New Testaments. The Old Testament focuses on God's love for us and on the ways in which we're commanded to return that love. In the Psalms, King David refers to God's love more than a hundred times. He writes often of God's "unfailing love" and his love that "endures forever." In the Proverbs, King Solomon tells us that the love of God is the beginning of wisdom.

Let love and faithfulness never leave you; bind them around your neck, write them on the tablet of your heart.

— Proverbs 3:3 NIV

The passages in the Old Testament that probably best sum up our command to love God and obey him are found in these words of Moses:

Love the Lord your God with all your heart and with all your soul and with all your strength.

— Deuteronomy 6:5 NIV

> *What does the Lord your God require of you except to*
> *listen carefully, to all he says to you, and to obey for your*
> *own good the commandments I am giving you today, and to*
> *love him, and to worship him with all your hearts and*
> *souls?*
>
> —DEUTERONOMY 10:12–13 TLB

Although the Old Testament puts greater emphasis on loving God and keeping his commandments than on loving one another, there are also eight references to the latter. The central message is expressed in this passage, also written by Moses:

> *Don't seek vengeance. Don't bear a grudge; but love your*
> *neighbor as yourself.*
>
> —LEVITICUS 19:18 TLB

The New Testament also contains several passages about loving God and honoring his commandments—the original ten and all the others spread throughout the Scriptures. The biggest difference between the two parts of the Bible is that the New Testament refers far more often to how we should treat one another: fellow believers, people of other faiths, nonbelievers, friends, spouses, children, the poor, the needy, sinners, even our enemies.

One of the central themes of the New Testament is encapsulated in Paul's first letter to his friends in Thessalonica:

> *May the Lord make your love increase and overflow for*
> *each other and for everyone else.*
>
> —1 THESSALONIANS 3:12 NIV

When he says to love *each other* he means fellow believers. That's usually easy because people who share the same faith and worship together have a lot in common and generally enjoy one another's company. But please notice that he also says our love should increase and overflow for *everyone else*. That pretty much takes in every person with whom we ever have contact. Loving all of them is not so easy. But here's an even greater challenge:

> *Love your enemies.*
> —Matthew 5:45 TLB

The word "enemy" conjures up several different thoughts, all of them unpleasant. It's important to understand that an enemy is not just an evil empire or person who wants to do harm to our country. That's one type of enemy, but the way I read this passage, it's not the one Matthew had in mind. The first definition of enemy in *Merriam-Webster* is "one that is antagonistic to another." It could be a person we strongly dislike, or it could be a person who dislikes us and often makes our lives unpleasant. We all have those kinds of people in our lives—at work, at school, sometimes within our families, and in a variety of public places. They irritate us, just as we occasionally irritate others. What are we to do with them? We're to love them. It's easy to love a friend; loving others is much harder work.

> *If you love only those who love you, what good is that?*
> *Even scoundrels do that much. If you are friendly to your*
> *friends, how are you different from anyone else?*
> —Matthew 5:46–47 TLB

So here are the two parts of the greatest challenge of all time:

1. Love everyone, including your enemies.
2. Do everything in love.

The first time I read the passages in the Bible that tell us to love everyone and to do everything in love, I honestly didn't think those commands were for regular people like me. I wasn't well versed in the Scriptures at the time and figured that verses like those were written only for people like the prophets, the apostles, the saints, and the martyrs—in other words, the *really* holy people. Possibly those could include people like C. S. Lewis, Albert Schweitzer, Billy Graham, Mother Teresa, and the pope, people who'd devoted their lives to God and to serving others and seem to be modern-day saints. We can't all be like them.

But as I studied and learned more about matters of faith and came to understand the Scriptures better, it became apparent that these passages, like all the others, were written for everyone, not just a special few. Most of us will never be able to write like C. S. Lewis, preach like Billy Graham, serve like Albert Schweitzer and Mother Teresa, or lead and inspire millions as Pope John Paul II did, but there are some things that we *can* do. We can love God, we can read the Scriptures, and we can apply their teachings to our lives. We may not be called to do the things these well-known holy people have done, but we *are* called to love others—everyone and at all times. Not easy, but not impossible either.

Anything is possible if you have faith.

—MARK 9:23 TLB

There are more than two hundred references to loving others in the New Testament. While I don't want to include all of them here, I do want to cite a few that seem to best capture the essence of the entire Bible's message: to love God and to love others. They also best capture the essential message of this book; we can make the world a far better one if we etch these two commands in our hearts and minds, and, more important, apply them in our daily lives.

Treat other people exactly as you would like to be treated—this is the essence of all true religion.

—MATTHEW 7:12 PHI

Love one another. In the same way I loved you, you love one another.

—JOHN 13:34 MES

If it is possible, as far as it depends on you, live at peace with everyone.

—ROMANS 12:18 NIV

Be humble and gentle. Be patient with each other, making allowances for each other's faults because of your love.

—EPHESIANS 4:2 TLB

Be kind to each other, be understanding.

—EPHESIANS 4:32 PHI

Be merciful in action, kindly in heart, humble in mind. Accept life, and be most patient and tolerant with one another, always ready to forgive if you have a difference with anyone. . . . And, above everything else, be truly loving, for love is the golden chain of all the virtues.

—COLOSSIANS 3:12–14 PHI

Never let your brotherly love fail, nor refuse to extend your hospitality to strangers.

—HEBREWS 13:1 PHI

Above all, love each other deeply, because love covers over a multitude of sins.

—1 PETER 4:8 NIV

Indeed all of you should defer to one another and wear the "overall" of humility in serving each other.

—1 PETER 5:5 PHI

As long as we love one another God remains in us and his love comes to its perfection in us.

—1 JOHN 4:12 JER

Love never fails.

—2 CORINTHIANS 13:8 NIV

ONE PERFECT DAY

A dear friend recently asked me what my new book was about. She was referring to my third book, *Choices That Change Lives*, which came out in January 2006. I replied with what leaped to mind: "It's about some very challenging stuff." It wasn't a very articulate answer, but it did capture the way I feel about the book's content. When she asked me what I meant, I said, "Let me tell you what the first five chapters are about: humility, patience, empathy, forgiveness, and giving. How's that for a challenge?" I was quick to point out that those five virtues are probably a greater challenge for the author than for most of his readers. She agreed that they were real tests of character.

We had a wonderful conversation about how life does challenge us daily, especially if we want to make the most of our time here on Earth. At one point she asked me if I was working on another book. I said, "Yes, about even *more* challenging stuff." Again not very articulate, but a true expression of my feelings. I told her that I thought the topics in this book pose a major challenge for almost all of us. And I think the last one, to do everything in love, is the greatest challenge of all.

Her next question nailed me: "Do you think you do everything in love?"

"Unfortunately, no," I had to tell her, "but I do a lot more things in love now than I used to. I guess now that I've written about it, I'll have to work even harder at it, because I'm still not up to the *everything* level."

After she left, I thought about the many times over the

course of my teaching career that I had issued one-day challenges to my students. Try, I'd asked them, to go one day:

Without complaining
Without criticizing anyone
Without saying anything negative

The challenges weren't limited to restraint. With the positive in mind, I'd also asked them to try to spend one day:

Giving their best in everything they did
Maintaining a positive attitude
Focusing on things to be thankful for

It occurred to me that I now had a new challenge before me—to spend one day doing everything in love. I'm not in the classroom any longer, so I have no students to challenge. If I made the challenge to the audience at one of my talks, they'd either think I was an aging San Francisco flower child or consider dialing 911 for information on the closest mental facility.

Then it dawned on me that I should challenge myself. At first I thought I'd do it on a day when I was home writing. I'd need to be loving to my wife, Cathy, in the morning before she went to work, and then again in the evening when she came home. I think I do pretty well at this, so it wouldn't be a big challenge. The only other time I'd need to be loving would be on the phone. Since most people who call during the day are either inviting me to speak or want to buy a bunch of books, it's always in my best interest to treat them lovingly. I decided I'd be selling myself short to take up the challenge on a day like that.

So I picked a day on which I would be speaking, driving, and flying, which is a challenge under any circumstances. I made up my mind when I got up in the morning that no matter what happened, and no matter how other people behaved, I would do everything in love. I knew I would have to repeat the phrase to myself several times throughout the day to keep from slipping into one of my ugly habits. I checked out of the hotel, filled the car with gas, drove to a school district, spoke to four hundred teachers in the morning and to a small group in the afternoon. Next I drove to the airport in Chicago, turned in the car, checked in, went through the security line, boarded the plane, flew home to San Francisco, collected my car, and drove home. It was a long, long day, during which I came into contact with hundreds of people, not all pleasant or even polite. It was, indeed, a challenge.

But as hectic and exhausting as the day was, there was something very special about it. I repeated the mantra "do everything in love" several times each hour—out of sheer necessity. And it worked! I always try to be polite and kind to people, but on this particular day I increased my concentration and my efforts in both areas. And throughout the long day I seemed to have more patience, more understanding, more empathy, more inner peace, and more joy than I could have imagined.

When I went to bed that night, I couldn't help thinking that it had been a virtually perfect day. For most people a perfect day is one during which everything goes right—there's no heavy traffic, everything runs on schedule, everyone is nice, work gets done smoothly, we have time to relax with friends, and so on. In other words, the kind of day we have is dependent upon outward circumstances over which we have no control. This little challenge from the Scriptures reminded me of something I already knew: it's not what happens to us, it's how we handle it. And the Scriptures tell us that the best way to handle everything is with love.

Of course, I'm embarrassed to admit that this is the first time I'd ever consciously tried to do everything in love. I'm sure I'm not alone. We read a passage from the Scriptures and nod our heads in agreement, then go on with life as usual. A friend and mentor once told me that we shouldn't just read the Bible; we should study it and ask ourselves a question: "How does this apply to my life?" Not only should we ask ourselves this question, we should work a little harder at applying these wise and great teachings to our lives.

If one day can be as good as the one I had putting a scriptural commandment into practice, why can't all of our days be equally good or even better? It's often been said that having a good life is having a whole bunch of good days in a row. The Scriptures tell us that the best way to string those days together is by doing everything in love.

> *Love doesn't make the world go round, love is what makes the ride worthwhile.*
>
> —ELIZABETH BARRETT BROWNING

> *To love is to receive a glimpse of heaven.*
>
> —KAREN SUNDE

> *Whatever someone sows, that is what he will reap.*
>
> —GALATIANS 6:7 JER

Conclusion: Love God, Be Good, Do Good, Love Others

A DEAR FRIEND recently asked me, "What are you writing about now?"

"The Scriptures." I can be succinct!

"Is it a Christian book?"

"Yes and no."

"Oh, thank you, that makes it really clear."

Detecting a hint of sarcasm, I said, "I'm actually trying to do the almost impossible—write a book about the Scriptures for people of all beliefs, including nonbelievers." Since she's a nonbeliever and unfamiliar with the Scriptures, my comment piqued her interest. She issued a little challenge of her own: "How would you describe the central message of the Scriptures in ten words or less?"

Succinct seemed to be the word of the day. Here's what I came up with: "Love God, be good, do good, love others."

"The last three sound fine, but I don't know about loving God. I don't even believe in God." I asked her if she believed there was some form of higher power or spiritual force that binds us all together.

"Oh, there is. I just don't know what name to give it." I suggested that for the sake of our conversation she call it God for the time being. She agreed to do that, and we went on to discuss life and its meaning, matters of the spirit, and our friendship. I couldn't help but circle back to beliefs, and I pointed out that believers and nonbelievers alike agree upon certain universal principles of conduct. No argument there. And I pointed out that the Scriptures contain all of them. She said she'd take my word on that and assured me that she would read this book.

Our conversation prompted me to closely examine the values and principles we all have in common, no matter what our faith and no matter what we believe. Here's the summary of my findings:

Moses, the first of the great prophets, fourteenth century B.C.:

> *Love your neighbor as yourself.*
> —Leviticus 19:18 NIV

King David, ruler of Israel, 1010–970 B.C.:

> *Turn from evil and do good; seek peace and pursue it.*
> —Psalm 34:14 NIV

A Greek philosopher who lived from 496 to 406 B.C.:

> *To be doing good is man's most glorious task.*
> —Sophocles

Saint Paul in the first century A.D.:

> *Let us not grow tired of doing good. . . .*
> *Let us do good to all men as opportunity offers.*
> —Galatians 6:9–10 PHI

A Protestant leader in the 1700s:

> *Do all the good you can, by all the means you can, in all the ways you can, in all the places you can, at all the times you can, to all the people you can, as long as ever you can.*
>
> —JOHN WESLEY

An American patriot and atheist of the Revolutionary period:

> *My religion is to do good.*
>
> —THOMAS PAINE

A famous Hindu civil rights leader:

> *I believe I am most likely to find God while I am serving others.*
>
> —MAHATMA GANDHI

A Nobel Peace Prize–winning Catholic nun:

> *Good works are links that form a chain of love. Spread love wherever you go. Let no one ever come to you without leaving happier.*
>
> —MOTHER TERESA

The leader of the Mormon Church:

> *The virtue of love changes lives—ours as well as those of everyone with whom we come in contact. It is the virtue that has embedded within its precincts the power to have the most lasting good.*

> *Love is the only force that can erase the differences*
> *between people or bridge the chasms of bitterness.*
> —GORDON B. HINCKLEY

A Nobel Peace Prize–winning Buddhist monk:

> *All major religious traditions carry basically the same*
> *message, that is love, compassion, and forgiveness . . . the*
> *important thing is they should be part of our daily lives.*
> —THE DALAI LAMA

A contemporary and highly acclaimed Jewish leader and author:

> *I believe that God made the human soul in such a way that*
> *certain kinds of behavior are healthier for us than others.*
> *Jealousy, selfishness, mistrust poison the soul; honesty,*
> *generosity, and cheerfulness restore it. We literally feel*
> *better after we have gone out of our way to be helpful to*
> *someone.*
>
> *God is the answer to the question, Why should I be a*
> *good and honest person when I see people around me*
> *getting away with murder? God is the answer not because*
> *He will intervene to reward the righteous and punish the*
> *wicked but because He has made the human soul in such a*
> *way that only a life of goodness and honesty leaves us feeling*
> *spiritually healthy and human.*
> —RABBI HAROLD KUSHNER

We Reap What We Sow

Let us not become weary in doing good, for at the proper time we will reap a harvest if we do not give up. . . . Therefore, as we have opportunity, let us do good to all people.

— Galatians 6:7,9–10 NIV

Books Cited

(in the order in which they appear)

The World's Religions by Huston Smith, HarperSanFrancisco, 1991.

The Road Less Traveled by M. Scott Peck, M.D., Simon & Schuster, 1978.

Man's Search for Meaning by Viktor E. Frankl, Beacon Press, 1959.

How to Get Control of Your Time and Your Life by Alan Lakein, Penguin Books, 1973.

First Things First by Stephen R. Covey, A. Roger Merrill, and Rebecca R. Merrill, Simon & Schuster, 1994.

Personal Finance for Dummies by Eric Tyson, IDG Books Worldwide, 2000.

Will Durant: The Greatest Minds and Ideas of All Time edited by John Little, Simon & Schuster, 2002.

Words That Hurt, Words That Heal by Rabbi Joseph Telushkin, William Morrow, 1996.

Illustrations of Bible Truth by H. A. Ironside, Moody Press, 1945.

The Anger Trap by Dr. Les Carter, John Wiley & Sons, 2003.

The Power of Patience by M. J. Ryan, Broadway Books, 2003.

Forgive for Good by Dr. Fred Luskin, HarperCollins Publishers, 2002.

Emotional Intelligence by Daniel Goleman, Bantam Books, 1995.

As a Man Thinketh by James Allen, Peter Pauper Press, c. 1905.

The Power of Positive Thinking by Norman Vincent Peale, Prentice-Hall, 1952.

When Bad Things Happen to Good People by Rabbi Harold Kushner, Avon Books, 1981.

The Power of Servant Leadership by Robert K. Greenleaf and Peter B. Vail, Barrett-Koehler Publishers, 1998.

Team of Rivals: The Political Genius of Abraham Lincoln by Doris Kearns Goodwin, Simon & Schuster, 2005.

How to Win Friends and Influence People by Dale Carnegie, Simon & Schuster, 1936.

The Art of Loving by Erich Fromm, Harper & Row Publishers, 1956.

Unconditional Love by John Powell, S.J., Argus Communications, 1978.

The Author's Spiritual Journey

A DEAR FRIEND recently told me that I should write a spiritual autobiography because he was moved by my evolving relationship with God. I would have used the word "painful" in there somewhere and told him so. I also said I wasn't important enough to write *any* kind of autobiography. But if I did, I know what I'd call it: "The Bumpy Road to Inner Peace." As briefly as I can put it, here's my story.

I was baptized a Catholic as an infant. I attended Mass regularly with my parents as a child and for eight years attended a Catholic elementary school, where I was taught by the Sisters of Mercy. We spent the first hour of each day learning history, prayers, and Catholic teachings before moving on to other subjects. I attended a public high school and continued to practice my faith conscientiously.

I then attended the University of San Francisco, a Jesuit institution. If you're unfamiliar with the Jesuits, they're probably best described as a teaching order of the Catholic Church founded by St. Ignatius Loyola. They place great emphasis on the teaching of theology, philosophy, logic, and ethics. I received an outstanding education and will always have a special place in my heart for the Jesuits. They taught me to think, and they taught me the importance of being an ethical person.

At the university I attended Mass and received Communion daily. I was often referred to as a "devout Catholic," and I was comfortable with that label. I remained one for the next eight years following graduation. Then things changed. Six and a half years into my marriage and three children later, my wife informed me that she was leaving. She divorced me and moved four hundred miles away with our three sons. I was powerless to prevent either the divorce or the separation from my children. It was devastating.

Along with the pain came some questions about God, my faith, and the rules of the Catholic Church. More than anything, I felt betrayed. How could God let something so horrible happen to a person who had honored him so consistently and so devoutly? In addition, I felt that Church doctrine prevented me from ever marrying again, so I would suffer because of another person's choices. That wasn't entirely correct, but it was my understanding at the time. In my anger and frustration I rejected both God and the Church.

For the next ten years I was an agnostic. But I did embrace a new religion: psychology. It all began when I started seeing a psychiatrist in order to cope with the pain of my divorce. I was reluctant to see a "shrink," but some dear friends who'd been through the same experience convinced me that it would help. And it did. In fact, I was amazed at how much it helped me deal with the pain, stop blaming myself, and move on with life. I was determined to learn as much about psychology as I could.

During those ten years I delved deeply into hundreds of psychology books, especially those written by leaders in the humanistic psychology movement of the 1970s. Psychologists like Abraham Maslow, Fritz Perls, Carl Rogers, Thomas Harris, and Virginia Satir became my gurus. I couldn't get enough of their books and of retreats, seminars, and workshops on becoming "self-actualized." I became the ultimate growth junkie. I frequently experienced rushes of euphoria and understanding, which convinced me I was on the right path—that I was truly "high on life."

The trouble was that those highs didn't last very long, and I was constantly on the lookout for the next fix. After several years, the whole process began to wear on me. The worst part was the emptiness I felt after a rush. The truth was, I was lonely and generally unhappy. Living for the next high really wasn't such a great way to live. A dear friend and mentor told me that I needed God back in my life. I figured that I had nothing to lose and that maybe I could reconnect with God outside the practice of Catholicism. There was a popular Protestant church in my area that he recommended, so I gave it a try. I knew the first time I attended that I did, in fact, need God back in my life.

I loved that church for several reasons: the fellowship, the pastors, and their deeper readings of the Scriptures. I also loved two policies that the church had. The pastors never said anything negative about another faith, and they kept politics out of the pulpit. I wish all places of worship had those same two policies. I became completely involved in this church, serving first as a deacon and later as an elder. I also frequently filled in for the main teachers in the Men's Bible Study classes, as I had become passionate about learning more about what the Scriptures were telling me. They were working a lot better than the humanistic psychology books and growth seminars had. I'm not sorry that I had those experiences, though, and I believe there's a place in our lives for faith and psychology.

After eighteen years I left that church for a simple reason—

the worship service ceased to feel like worship. Each year that I was there the Sunday service became a bigger and bigger production. Some members of the congregation began to refer to it as "The Show," and it did seem more like entertainment than worship. So I tried another church, a nondenominational one with an incredibly articulate, funny pastor who knew the Bible well. I loved it at first, but that same feeling that the service was more about showmanship than worship crept up on me again. To make it worse, the pastor openly criticized other churches from the pulpit. I began to long for the reverence of the Catholic Mass: the quiet prayer time, the kneelers (the best possible position in which to pray), the sound of voices united as we said the Lord's Prayer while joining hands, receiving the Sacraments.

But could I go back to the Catholic Church? I had been away from the Church for thirty-two years, and a lot had changed. I spent a long time with the pastor of the parish near my home, did a lot of reading, listened to several tapes by Catholic scholars, and talked for hours with Catholics who are devout Christians and outstanding role models. They have a close personal relationship with God, and they consistently put the teachings of the Scriptures into practice.

My decision to return was made easier by my knowing that it wasn't a matter of making a choice between Catholic and Protestant. I knew I could benefit from the teachings of each. I will be eternally grateful for those twenty-two years I spent in Protestant churches. I wouldn't be writing this book if I hadn't had that experience. Most Protestant churches do an excellent job of helping people understand the Bible and of encouraging its study. They also do a good job of helping people develop a personal relationship with God. It's a simple concept, but important.

I see the great strengths of the Catholic Church as its history (including the Reformation), its teachings, traditions, and rituals; the reverence of the Mass; the Sacraments; its devotion to the poor and charitable work; its schools and colleges; the lives and writings of the saints; the liturgical calendar; and, yes, the kneelers.

There's an important point to be made here. Where a person goes to worship for an hour on the Sabbath each week isn't what determines whether he or she is a Christian or anything else. Going into my garage doesn't make me a car, and going into a church doesn't make me a Christian. That's determined by my personal relationship with God and my desire and willingness to live according to his teachings.

Because I've spent many years in both Catholic and Protestant churches, I feel comfortable in both. I can even speak the language of each. Yes, they do talk a little differently. I also appreciate what each has to offer. I currently attend Mass on Saturday evening and go with my wife, Cathy, to her Protestant church on Sunday morning. I get different things out of each service, almost all of them good.

Chances are I'm offending a conservative Catholic reader out there somewhere who's thinking that if I'm Catholic, I shouldn't attend a Protestant service. Some of them have misconceptions about Protestants and what they believe. And there are likely to be some conservative Protestants reading this who are disappointed that I returned to worship in a Catholic church. Some of them have misconceptions about Catholics and what they believe. They have their differences, no doubt, but I worship the same God in both places.

Thank You

WRITING CAUSES ME to seriously question my sanity. Some of the words associated with it, at least in this author's mind, are "slow," "painful," "frustrating," "lonely," and "agonizing." It often makes me wonder if I have some masochistic tendencies. Why do I put myself through this torture? It's only when I get to this favorite part of the book that I come up with the answer. I do it because some very special people tell me that my work has significance and meaning, that it touches people's lives. They also help me through the process with their encouragement, ideas, suggestions, their own hard work, and, most important, their friendship. There are no words in our language that can express the true depth of my appreciation for these people, but I need at least to try.

Don McClean: In the first two pages I wrote about this wonderful man, who's been a colleague, friend, and mentor for close to forty years. He helped me redirect and resurrect my life after it hit bottom in the late 1970s. He did it by steering me back to my faith, by helping me understand it more fully, and by teaching me about the wonders of the Scriptures. This book would not have been possible without Don's love, friendship, and wisdom.

Cathy Urban: As she's done in the past, my wife, Cathy, has given me invaluable help in several ways. From beginning to end she's been there with encouragement, insight, gentle criticism, and constructive advice. Equally appreciated is her understanding when I don't come out of my "cave" for long periods at a time.

Chris Lloreda: I often wonder if any other author has an associate publisher who so effectively combines intelligence, professionalism, warmth, integrity, enthusiasm, and humor. Chris is all these and more and has been there every step of the way since I became a Simon & Schuster author in 2002. I've never had another colleague who's made me laugh more or made me feel more appreciated, who's added so much joy to my life.

Trish Todd: It was my good fortune to be in frequent contact with Trish throughout the writing of this book. As editorial director, she stepped in when the Fireside division of S&S came up one editor short. Despite her many administrative responsibilities, she was always there with the right answers, any help that I needed, and wholehearted support for the book. On top of all this, she found a wonderful editor for me.

Lisa Considine: When Trish told me that Lisa would be working with me on the manuscript of the book, she said, "You'll like her. She's a kind soul and an outstanding editor." Both were understatements. It's been an absolute delight working with her. A good editor makes an author look better than he really is. She's done that on almost every page of this book, and I'm deeply appreciative.

My readers: I can't count the number of people who've written, telephoned, and e-mailed me regarding my three previous books. Their stories, their pain, their joy, their insights, their expressions of appreciation, and their suggestions have all touched me deeply. A large percentage of these people have thanked me for always getting right to the point, for explaining things simply, and for showing so much common sense. All of this has had more influence on my writing than they'll ever know, and the title of this book is in large part a tribute to them. Thank you.

About the Author

Hal Urban holds bachelor's and master's degrees in history and a doctorate in education and psychology from the University of San Francisco. He has also done postgraduate study in the psychology of peak performance at Stanford University.

For thirty-five years he was an award-winning teacher at both the high school and university levels. His first book, *Life's Greatest Lessons,* was selected as "Inspirational Book of the Year" by *Writer's Digest.*

Since 1992, Dr. Urban has been speaking nationally and internationally on positive character traits and their relationship to the quality of life. He gives keynote addresses at national conferences, conducts workshops with educators, and talks to students of all ages. He also speaks to parents, church groups, service organizations, and people in business.

In 2005, Dr. Urban was presented the Sanford N. McDonnell Lifetime Achievement Award at the Character Education Partnership National Forum.

Information about his lectures and workshops can be obtained by contacting him in one of the following ways:

Web site: **www.halurban.com**
E-mail: **halurban@halurban.com**
Phone: (650) 366-0882

More powerful ways to enrich your life and the lives of others, from Hal Urban.

HAL URBAN

More than a quarter million copies sold

LIFE'S GREATEST LESSONS

"With its timeless message for people of all ages . . . it should be in every home in America." —KEN BLANCHARD, coauthor of *The One Minute Manager*

20 THINGS THAT MATTER

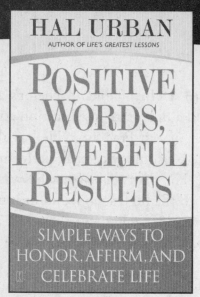

HAL URBAN

AUTHOR OF *LIFE'S GREATEST LESSONS*

POSITIVE WORDS, POWERFUL RESULTS

SIMPLE WAYS TO HONOR, AFFIRM, AND CELEBRATE LIFE

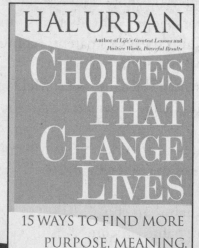

HAL URBAN

Author of *Life's Greatest Lessons* and *Positive Words, Powerful Results*

CHOICES THAT CHANGE LIVES

15 WAYS TO FIND MORE PURPOSE, MEANING, AND JOY

HAL URBAN

Mas de un cuarto de millon de ejemplares vendidos

Las grandes lecciones de la vida

«Este libro contiene un mensaje que trasciende todos los tiempos y es válido para personas de todas las edades... Debería estar en cada hogar». —KEN BLANCHARD, coautor de *The One Minute Manager*

APRENDIENDO LO QUE ES REALMENTE IMPORTANTE A PARTIR DE LA EXPERIENCIA

Available wherever books are sold or at www.simonsays.com

SIMON & SCHUSTER
LIBROS EN ESPAÑOL

FIRESIDE
A Division of Simon & Schuster
A CBS COMPANY